HISTORY OF THE 12TH (SERVICE) BATTALION YORK & LANCASTER REGIMENT.

[Photo W. H. Babington.

Colonel C. V. Mainwaring.

HISTORY of the 12th SERVICE BATTALION YORK & LANCASTER REGIMENT

Richard·A·Sparling

The Naval & Military Press Ltd

Reproduced by kind permission of the Central Library,
Royal Military Academy, Sandhurst

Published by
The Naval & Military Press Ltd
Unit 10 Ridgewood Industrial Park,
Uckfield, East Sussex,
TN22 5QE England
Tel: +44 (0) 1825 749494
Fax: +44 (0) 1825 765701
www.naval-military-press.com
www.military-genealogy.com
www.militarymaproom.com

In reprinting in facsimile from the original, any imperfections are inevitably reproduced and the quality may fall short of modern type and cartographic standards.

TO

THE SILENT HEROES

OF THE

SHEFFIELD CITY BATTALION

WHO GAVE THEIR LIVES

THAT BRITAIN AND HER EMPIRE

MIGHT LIVE.

Contents.

CHAPTER		PAGE
I.	ANSWERING THE CALL	1
II.	DAYS OF AULD LANG SYNE	8
III.	THE EARLY DAYS ABROAD	18
IV.	FRANCE AT LAST!	26
V.	THE BAPTISM OF FIRE	33
VI.	EVE OF THE SOMME BATTLE	47
VII.	THE GALLANT FIGHT FOR SERRE	55
VIII.	STRANGE INCIDENTS AND A WINTER'S TALE	75
IX.	THE ADVANCE ON PUISIEUX	88
X.	ADVENTURES ON VIMY RIDGE	99
XI.	STORMY DAYS OF BLACK MICHAEL	.. 116

Illustrations.

Colonel C. V. Mainwaring ..	*Frontispiece.*

	FACING PAGE
Colonel H. Hughes, C.B., C.M.G.	4
The Right Hon. H. A. L. Fisher, Minister of Education	12
Early days at Bramall Lane	20
Listening to the late Colonel Hughes' motto: " Work, Work, Work ! "	28
Marching to the Redmires Camp in 1914	36
On the march—Old Familiar Faces !	44
The Civic Farewell at the Town Hall, May 13th, 1915 .	52
El Ferdan Station and the Suez Canal	60
The good ship " Nestor " proceeding down Suez Canal	60
Sketch of the trenches where the City Battalion men fell on July 1st, 1916	64
The Sucrerie, Serre	68
A scene in Ecurie, near Arras .	76
One of the first trenches the Battalion entered in 1916, Near Serre Road	
Lieut.-Col. J. A. Crosthwaite, the late Lieut.-Col. H. B. Fisher, Lieut.-Col. C. P. B. Riall, and Lieut.-Col. F. J. Courteney Hood, D.S.O.	84
Hon. Lieut. and Quartermaster R. Polden, M.C.	92
Hebuterne, 1916	92

Illustrations.

	FACING PAGE
A view of Lens, the great mining centre in the North of France	100
The scene of the Cadorna attack of 1917	108
An aeroplane view of country before it has been devastated by shell fire	116
After the guns have spoken	116
The Memorial in the Sheffield Cathedral ..	145

PREFACE.

ANYONE who shoulders the responsibility of endeavouring to present the history of a battalion during the Great War is accepting a heavy and difficult task, for the complexities are many and varied. However, in presenting this volume on the Sheffield City Battalion, I think that a much-needed want is being filled. I have taken the greatest care to give a faithful and accurate record of a noble Battalion, in which I had the privilege of serving during the whole of its existence.

Many will say that they do not require any book to remind them of what the Sheffield City Battalion did in the Great War; of the awful sacrifice of July 1st, 1916; but be it said that memories fail and colours fade.

Again, the heroism of those who fell deserves a lasting recognition such as this is intended to be. In numerous instances, alas! it may be the only link with a loved one now departed.

It occurred to me that it might, perhaps, add value to the volume as a memorial to old comrades if it were briefly mentioned that the notes and records which have made it possible to tell this story were in many instances preserved only with considerable difficulty. They have survived tremendous ordeals; they have jogged along in a knapsack for hundreds of miles across some of the famous battlefields, including the Somme, Vimy Ridge, Passchendaele, and Ypres, and their fate was in the balance during the terrific clashes of arms in 1918.

There are shortcomings, I know, but to those who would point out the omissions, I should like to say that a sense of proportion had to be maintained and that this is a history of a battalion and not a collection of personal anecdotes only.

I am greatly indebted to Mr. Howard R. Sleigh for a contribution to the chapter on the battle for Serre, and for his gift of the chapters dealing with the Battalion's progress in England. I also have to acknowledge the courtesy of the Officer in charge Infantry Records, No. 2, York, and Mr. J. Melling, for the provision of the Roll of Honour; and the assistance, in the illustration section, of Directors of the Imperial War Museum, the Director of Publicity at the War Office, Major A. Plackett, Captain E. L. Moxey, Mr. L. Beaumont, Mr. F. Ratcliffe, F.R.I.B.A., and Mr. J. R. Rodinson. In addition, I must express gratitude to Professor G. C. Moore Smith, Litt.D. (St. John's College, Cambridge), Hon. Ph.D. Louvain), of the Sheffield University; and Mr. J. S. Wood, for valuable advice.

                        RICHARD A. SPARLING.

Sheffield,
    February 23rd, 1920.

Chapter One.
Answering the Call.

The good-looking crowd: Falling in: Bramall Lane joys: Extended order drill in Norfolk Park: the notable supper.

EVEN for remarkable times, it was a remarkable scene which presented itself at the Norfolk Barracks, Sheffield, one sultry afternoon in the September of 1914. Six weeks earlier, Europe had been plunged into war. There were still vast numbers of people in this country who failed to understand what it meant for England. But in this hall were a thousand men of Sheffield who understood, and who had given up their homes, their professions and their businesses, to form an entirely new regiment within a few days—ready to take their share in the battle.

"You are a crowd; a good-looking crowd, but a CROWD," their Commanding Officer told them, as he leaned over the balcony and gave them for their motto the word "Work."

Sans uniform, formed up anyhow, the Sheffield Battalion looked a crowd. But they were an unusual crowd, one such as had not been seen in England before the Great War. Their ages ranged from 19 to 35. Standing there as privates were many men whom no other conceivable circumstances would have brought into the Army; £500 a year business men, stockbrokers, engineers, chemists, metallurgical experts, University and public school men, medical students, journalists, schoolmasters, craftsmen, shop assistants, secretaries, and all sorts of clerks.

They were a strange mixture from the trained soldier's point of view. And yet a well-set-up, strapping lot for the most part, who might perhaps have pleased an old recruiting sergeant's eye. They represented ore of which it might be hoped that the fire of military training would make well-tempered stuff.

The men who took part in that first parade are not likely to forget it. Memorable speeches were made by well-known Sheffield citizens who had worked to raise the battalion. Moreover, the place seemed only just big enough to hold the "crowd." For two and a half hours they moved about under the orders of first one, and then another, while attempts were made to create some little order out of a vast amount of chaos.

Each man stuck to his particular friends, and of the making of lists there was no end. Finally a number of temporary squads were arranged. The leaders were selected by the late Colonel Hughes, from the Sheffield University men who had had O.T.C. training, and the ex-Regulars, Territorials and Volunteers who had joined. Then the men were dismissed for the day.

Having thus given a rough idea of the first parade, which took place on Monday, September 14th, 1914, let us see how it was that the Battalion came to be formed.

About the 1st September, 1914, the late Duke of Norfolk, E.M., K.G., and the late Sir George Franklin, Litt.D., J.P., representing the University of Sheffield, attended at the War Office, and suggested the formation of a local battalion in Sheffield on the lines already adopted in certain other Cities, the general idea being that a Unit should be provided in which Sheffield University and commercial men could enlist together, and have some special connection with their own city.

They were received favourably at the War Office, and Sir G. Franklin communicated the result of their interview to the then Lord Mayor of Sheffield, Lieut.-Colonel G. E. Branson, J.P., with a view to obtaining official municipal recognition and assistance in the formation of the Battalion.

The Lord Mayor called a meeting which was held at the Town Hall, on the 1st September, 1914, and was attended by the Duke of Norfolk, Sir G. Franklin, Sir William Clegg, Col. H. Hughes, C.B., C.M.G., and Mr. H. A. L. Fisher, the Vice-Chancellor of the University, at which it was arranged

Answering the Call.

that a Battalion—whose first official title should be "The Sheffield University and City Special Battalion of the York and Lancaster Regiment"—should forthwith be raised.

Colonel Hughes offered his services as Commanding Officer, and was requested to take the position of Acting Commandant until a Commanding Officer should be appointed by the War Office.

Captain E. A. Marples, late of the 4th (Hallamshire) Battalion, Y. and L. Regiment (T.F.), who had had South African war experience, was requested to act as temporary Adjutant.

Surgeon-Captain W. S. Kerr, of the same Battalion, consented to act as temporary Medical Officer.

A little later Major T. Carter Clough, V.D., also of the same Battalion, was invited to accept a temporary Commission.

Recruiting began in the first instance by a process of enrolment. This took place in one of the Reception Rooms at the Town Hall. Fifteen hundred forms of declaration of willingness to serve were prepared, and within a few days some 1,400 names were handed in to the Lord Mayor and the officers who assisted him.

Arrangements were then made for the formal enlistment at the Corn Exchange, the men who had enrolled being asked to attend there. Enlistment began on the 10th September, and a very big but on the whole well-handled task it proved.

"To Berlin—via Corn Exchange," said the placards, and the men came in their hundreds, to undergo the long cross-examination of the manifold attestation clerks, followed by the medical examination of the small army of doctors who very cheerily gave their valuable help. When a man came from behind the doctor's screens smiling, you knew without asking that he had been passed fit for the service of his country.

Rejections, chiefly on medical grounds, were, however, somewhat numerous, and during the two days on which it had been expected to recruit up to strength, between 900 and 1,000 men only were enlisted. But other men were soon forthcoming.

History of The Sheffield City Battalion.

The honour of being the first recruit to enrol at the Town Hall belonged to the late Captain V. S. Simpson, M.C., who, unfortunately, was killed in action at Vieux Berquin, in April, 1918, in the battle of the Lys, when the enemy was bent on forcing a passage to the Channel Ports.

The first home of the Battalion was Norfolk Barracks, Edmund Road, Sheffield, previously best known to the majority of the men, probably, as a favourite place for boxing contests. The loan of the place was kindly granted by the West Riding Territorial Force Association.

A preliminary list of proposed officers was drawn up by Colonel Hughes and submitted to the Lord Mayor and Sir G. Franklin, who after making such changes as seemed necessary, arranged for the temporary employment of the gentlemen named, as officers of the Battalion. This list contained the following:—

Officer Commanding: Colonel H. Hughes, C.B., C.M.G.
Second in Command: Major T. Carter Clough, V.D.
Adjutant: Captain E. A. Marples.
Captains: A. R. Hoette, A. Plackett, W. A. Colley, Captain and Hon. Major W. J. Armitage.
Lieutenants: C. F. Ellwood, W. J. Jarrard, J. Kenner, A. N. Cousin, C. Elam, E. G. G. Woolhouse, J. L. Middleton, G. Beley.
Second Lieutenants: N. L. Tunbridge, E. L. Moxey, R. E. J. Moore, G. J. H. Ingold, W. S. Clark.
Quartermaster: Hon. Lieut. S. W. Maunder.

Further officers were appointed from time to time on the nomination of the Commanding Officer for the time being.

The Lord Mayor and Sir G. Franklin were informed by the War Office that they were desired to be responsible for the organization, administration, and training of the Battalion until it was taken over by the War Office.

The day after the " mobilization parade " already described, the Battalion got to work on squad drill. For this there was at first available a splendid level area in the shape of the Sheffield United Cricket and Football Club's famous home at Bramall Lane—a resort of sporting Sheffielders for decades past, and one which had witnessed

Colonel H. Hughes, C.B., C.M.G.

Answering the Call.

many feats of physical prowess by sturdy Yorkshiremen. No one had ever thought it would one day present such a sight as now.

During the first fortnight the Battalion employed a certain number of old soldiers as paid drill instructors, but it was soon found that the necessary material could be found for instruction within the ranks.

The Battalion was, indeed, particularly fortunate in the possession of a number of ex-N.C.O.'s and men of the Regular Forces—pensioners, time-expired men, and others. Some had served in India with the York and Lancaster Regiment, and so were able to bring in something of the traditions of the old 65th and 84th Foot. Others had been in the Guards. One of these declared that the Battalion was as advanced in its work after three weeks' training as ordinary recruits would have been after three months, and thereby pleased them greatly besides raising wild hopes of an early appearance at "The Front," which were afterwards to be dashed.

Even Bramall Lane was hardly big enough for the requirements of the Battalion. When it was found that drill was cutting short the career of the grass, the directors reduced the size of the space available for work. Other grounds were used—pieces in Edmund Road and Queen's Road—and the regiment received its first education in extended order drill and attack on days which were really rather jolly, among the trees of Norfolk Park. This will be a memorable place to many a man as being where he set his foot on the ladder of promotion, winning his first stripe by the ordeal of drilling a platoon before the C.O.

For nearly three months the men lived at their own homes. Those who came from the outside districts were generously provided by Sheffield householders with lodgings either free or very cheaply. During this period the Battalion received its first uniform. This was of dark blue-grey cloth, khaki being unobtainable. The cap was small, of a modified F.S. or Glengarry pattern, and smartened by a thin red stripe.

On November 9th the Battalion was inspected by Field-Marshal H. Plumer, General Officer Commanding-in-Chief, Northern Command.

History of The Sheffield City Battalion.

At this point one should refer to changes which took place during the early existence of the Battalion. It had barely been raised a month when Colonel C. V. Mainwaring, Indian Army, was appointed by the War Office to the command, the date of his taking over from Colonel Hughes being October 10th, 1914. Another change about this time occurred in the departure of the acting Adjutant, Captain Marples, who was gazetted to the 13th Service Battalion of the Northumberland Fusiliers.

Captain and Hon. Major W. J. Armitage, who had been appointed to command what was called " No. 1 Double Company," left to take up a position in his old regiment, the Hallamshires.

Lieutenant E. G. G. Woolhouse became Adjutant, a position which he held until January, 1915, and upon his resigning the appointment it was given to Lieutenant N. L. Tunbridge.

The advisability of removing the men to camp was early considered. Authority was obtained from the War Office to put the Battalion into hutments, and in this connection it should be mentioned that during the whole period of the formation and equipment of the Battalion the late Sir G. Franklin, who was in London, greatly assisted the regiment by keeping in constant touch with the War Office and ascertaining the views of the authorities as to the housing, clothing, and training of the men.

As the camp site, an extensive area of moorland at Redmires, five or six miles on the Derbyshire side of Sheffield, was chosen. This had previously formed an old racecourse, and was later used by the W.R. Divisional Artillery (T.F.). The rent was £100 per annum.

It was a lofty spot—one of the highest camping grounds in England, in fact. Inclined to marshiness and swept by all the winter storms, it presented its own difficulties in the preparation of a camp, and the move of the Battalion could not take place as early as had been anticipated. The contracts for the erection of the hutments were entered into under directions from the War Office, and much able assistance was given in the work by the City Architect, Mr. F. E. P. Edwards.

Answering the Call.

Meanwhile contracts for the provision of clothing and necessaries, equipment, and barrack furniture were entered into by the Lord Mayor with various tradesmen, and the goods were supplied independently of the War Office.

Prior to the departure of the Battalion from the city they were addressed at a special service in St. Mary's Church, by the vicar of the parish, the Rev. Canon W. J. Cole. The men marched through the city afterwards, and created a good impression.

Another event in connection with the move, which was likewise a great success, was a supper given to the Battalion by Sir Samuel Roberts, M.P. It took place at Norfolk Barracks on 26th November.

Saturday, December 5th, witnessed the departure for camp. The strength of the Battalion was then 1,131, including thirty officers, one warrant officer, and sixty-seven N.C.O.'s.

Chapter Two.
Days of Auld Lang Syne.

Redmires: The hardening process: A great sports meeting: Rugeley and Ripon: The famous Marching Song: Forming the reserves: On Salisbury Plain: The last days in England.

THE day of the move to Redmires was wild and stormy. A steady fall of snow and rain did not make a very pleasant introduction to a camp which still needed a vast amount of attention to be made at all desirable. For a long time the weather continued bad. The regiment had every chance to make itself wonderfully fit physically by a considerable experience of quarrying, roadmaking, and so on.

As might be expected, this was not an aspect of military life which created any great joy at the time among the soft-handed men who made up the regiment. It has also to be admitted that the regimental cooks had to learn their business, and one never knew when a catastrophe was going to happen to the breakfast. Between one thing and another there were some rather exciting times until matters settled down. But later on the men came to look back upon the Redmires days as some of the happiest of their lives.

It was here that they really laid the foundation of their military training. And there is no doubt that Redmires served them magnificently with a case-hardening process which was of the greatest value in their training. The result of their hard graft, in all weathers, on the surrounding hills and moors was seen very clearly later on, when they could out-march the other regiments with which they were associated, and triumph over rivals in athletic events.

Days of Auld Lang Syne.

For just over five months the regiment remained at Redmires Camp, and the period witnessed a great deal of progress in training and various notable events.

A week or two before Christmas the regiment was placed in the 115th Infantry Brigade, together with the 10th (S.) Battalion Lincolnshire Regiment (Grimsby) and the 13th and 14th (S.) Battalions York and Lancaster Regiment (1st and 2nd Barnsleys), under the command of Brigadier-General H. Bowles, C.B., who had his headquarters first in Bank Street, Sheffield, and later in Brunswick Street, Sheffield. The 115th Infantry Brigade formed part of the 5th New Army. On April 10th the Reserve Company, " E " Company, moved into camp.

On April 29th the parade ground at Redmires was the scene of a great Regimental Sports meeting. Despite the distance from Sheffield, there were probably 10,000 spectators, and the exhibition of the Sheffield Battalion's sporting prowess was favourably commented upon. A day later the Battalion was inspected for the second time by the General Officer Commanding-in-Chief, Northern Command. In the long interval between this inspection and the first, Field-Marshal Plumer had left to fight in France, and had handed over the Northern Command to Major-General H. Lawson. General Lawson was very complimentary indeed, regarding the smart appearance of the Battalion and the cleanliness of the camp.

On Sunday, May 9th, Colonel Mainwaring received directions to prepare for the removal of the regiment from Redmires to Cannock Chase on May 13th. This was great news, and flew round the camp like wildfire. Everybody worked with a will. The stores, kits, &c., were early packed and dispatched. While this was going on intimation was received that the 115th Brigade had been renumbered as the 94th and placed in the Fourth Army, while there was a change in its constitution, the 11th (S.) East Lancashire Battalion being introduced vice the 10th (S.) Battalion Lincolnshire Regiment.

The unfortunate thing about the change of quarters was that it meant the departure of " Sheffield's Own " without Sheffield being given a fair opportunity of seeing the men off. The railway authorities fixed a very early hour for the move, and the Battalion had to parade at 5 a.m. to get to the station in time.

This notwithstanding, a great number of people turned out to see them. The Hallamshires' and R.E. bands played them through the city. From a platform erected on the Surrey Street side of the Town Hall they were addressed by the Lord Mayor (Councillor O. C. Wilson), Colonel Branson, and others, then marched on to the station through crowds of relatives and friends. For miles after leaving the city the men were responding to the cheers of folk who had taken up positions near the railway line.

The strength of the Battalion (excluding the reserve company, " E," which was left at Redmires) was at this time as follows: 34 officers, 6 warrant officers, 41 sergeants, 40 corporals and other ranks, making up a total of 1,104.

The move to Cannock Chase, with the consequent concentration of the 94th Brigade—which formed a part of the 31st Division, Fourth New Army—meant, of course, an advance in the stage of training of all its Battalions; though owing to the amount of fatigue work which was found necessary, the advance was not so great as it might have been. The brigade was encamped at Penkridge Bank Camp, on a high part of the Chase, near the little market town of Rugeley. The 94th Brigade was the first to move into this camp, which grew marvellously all the time it was there. The surrounding moorland, where the deer still roamed wild, formed a useful training sphere. The men of the Sheffield Battalion soon made themselves popular in the neighbouring towns of Stafford, Rugeley, Cannock, &c., and the records prove that they were entitled to their full share of the credit for a resolution which was passed by the Rugeley Urban District Council, on the Brigade's departure for a new field of action, conveying compliments as to the behaviour of its members.

A good deal of route marching was done here, and combined brigade operations became a regular feature of the work done. On 13th July, 1915, there was a full parade of the Sheffield Battalion for inspection prior to the formal taking over of the regiment by the War Office from the care of its original raisers.

Days of Auld Lang Syne.   11

Towards the end of the month came the long-expected order to move to the Divisional Headquarters at Ripon. Colonel Mainwaring was on sick leave at this time, and the regiment moved, with Major T. Carter Clough in command, on the night 30-31 July, leaving its huts and lines in a state which elicited the highest praise from those concerned. There is little need to dwell at length upon the trying march to Stafford, which exhausted almost every member of the Battalion and led to much heart-burning; suffice it to say, it will never be forgotten. The town of Rugeley gave the Battalion a great send-off.

The very fine camp at Ripon, on the Harrogate Road, was, naturally, with the headquarters of the 4th Army Training Centre close at hand, the scene of important fresh work for the Battalion. New courses of instruction for all ranks were entered upon, and, beginning on August 17th, the Battalion fired its preliminary Musketry Course, using the eighty short M.L.E. rifles which had been issued for the purpose.

General Sir Bruce Hamilton, commanding the 4th A.T.C., carried out an inspection of the Battalion, with its transport, &c., on August 4th; while it was also inspected by Major-General Sir A. J. Murray, Deputy C.I.G.S., on the 11th of the same month.

Major-General R. Wanless O'Gowan, C.B., who took over command of the 31st Division on 24th August from Major-General E. A. Fanshawe, C.B., inspected the Battalion on September 8th, and expressed himself as extremely pleased with the physique and turn-out of the regiment and the smartness with which they handled their arms.

It was now known that the Brigade was about to make probably its last move before leaving England—that was, to Salisbury Plain—and all ranks were granted four clear days' leave prior to leaving Yorkshire; a privilege which was very welcome. While the first half of the Battalion were enjoying this spell of holiday, the rest were celebrating in camp the anniversary of the raising of the Battalion, September 10th.

About this time the following officers were transferred from the Service Companies to the Depot: 2nd Lieut. W. A. Tyzack, 2nd Lieut. H. D. Reeve, 2nd Lieut. D. A. L. Derry.

2nd Lieut. F. A. Beal joined the Service Companies on transfer from the Manchester Regiment.

The Regimental March was that of the 2nd Battalion of the York and Lancaster Regiment, to which many of the chief ex-Regular N.C.O.'s of the City Battalion had belonged—" Jock o' York."

Prime favourite among the many songs that were sung upon the march was a strange folk-song of which no one seemed to know the origin. The honour of introducing it was generally given to the men from the Penistone district, and it first became well known at the Cannock Chase Camp. It had a fine swinging melody, said to be that of an old-fashioned hymn. The words were:

ON ILKLEY MOOR BAR'T'AT.

(1) Wheer has't a been sin' I saw thee?
Wheer has't a been sin' I saw thee?
Wheer has't a been sin' I saw thee?
(Chorus)   On Ilkley Moor bar't'at!
On Ilkley Moor bar't'at!
On Ilkley Moor bar't'at!
(2) Tha's been a coortine' our Sar' Ann;
Tha's been, &c.
(3) That's wheer thee'll ketch thee death o' cold;
That's wheer, &c.
(4) Then we shall have to bury thee;
Then we, &c.
(5) Then worms will come an' ate thee up; &c.
(6) Then ducks will come an' ate them worms; &c.
(7) Then we shall come an' ate ducks up; &c.
(8) (Fortissimo) That's wheer we gets us own back! &c.

As most of the Battalion themselves needed information as to the meaning of the chief phrase in the song, one would add that it is " On Ilkley Moor without a hat! "

The Battalion's first rifles consisted of twenty-three, which were kindly lent by Messrs. Vickers, Ltd., shortly after the formation. These proved invaluable for early instructional work. Another favour done by Messrs. Vickers, Ltd., through the kindness of Mr. Clark, was the loan of a machine gun, which enabled machine-gun training to be commenced months before this would have otherwise been the case.

The Right Hon. H. A. L. FISHER, Minister of Education.

(The idea of the Battalion came from two students of the University, and in consequence, Mr. Fisher, then Vice-Chancellor of the University, approached the Lord Mayor of Sheffield, Colonel Branson. Thus Mr. Fisher should be recognized as the moving force which led to the Battalion's formation).

Days of Auld Lang Syne. 13

Rifles of the M.L.M. pattern were received as under:

22nd October, 1914...	200
27th October, 1914...	200
31st October, 1914...	200
21st June, 1915 ...	1,000
	1,600

Through various causes 1,000 of these rifles had to be returned between the 9th of May, 1915, and June 10th, 1915, but on June 21st, 1915, 500 of those given up were returned, making the complement of rifles up to 1,100. Many of these were in bad condition, but fit to fire from and for drill purposes. On the 17th June, 1915, eighty M.L.E. (short) rifles were received for instructional purposes and were issued to N.C.O.'s.

All the 1914 pattern accoutrements were obtained from Messrs. Hepburn, Gale and Ross, Bermondsey, and the regiment was fully equipped by the end of February.

The undermentioned gentlemen of Sheffield presented the battalion drums: Colonel Hughes, C.B., C.M.G., big drum; Messrs. A. J. Hobson, W. Hobson, A. Wightman, and S. J. Robinson, side drums.

Sir Charles Allen presented fifes and cardholders.

Sir Samuel Roberts, M.P., presented the Union Jack to fly over Redmires Camp, and renewed it when the first one had been destroyed by the winter gales.

As to equipment in general, the Battalion was deeply indebted to the late Sir George Franklin and Colonel Branson for their untiring energy and assistance in providing everything that was needed.

Hardly coming under the heading of equipment, but at the same time assisting a great deal in the training of the Battalion at Redmires, was the loan by Mr. Wilson, of Beauchief Hall, of a portion of his land near the camp for the purpose of trench digging.

The question of providing reinforcements for local battalions was dealt with by the War Office within three months of the Battalion's formation, authority for the raising of a Fifth Company being received early in December.

14   History of The Sheffield City Battalion.

The new company was placed under the command of Captain G. Beley, and recruiting was carried on at the Town Hall, Sheffield, beginning in the third week of December. The men were billeted at their own homes, as the original members of the Battalion had been, while fresh accommodation was provided at Redmires. Drilling on fine days was carried out in Norfolk Park, and on wet days in a building called " The Jungle," previously a skating rink, in Hawley Street.

On April 10th, 1915, the Fifth, or " E " Company, moved into Redmires Camp. The company on that date was 224 strong, apart from officers. It did not reach its establishment of 250 until towards the end of May. When the Service companies left Redmires for Staffordshire the Fifth Company remained behind, under the command of Captain Beley, who had the following officers: Captain J. Kenner, 2nd Lieut. N. O. Lucas, 2nd Lieut. J. S. Cooper, and 2nd Lieut. V. S. Simpson.

Directly after the Service companies' change of station authority was received for raising the Sixth Company.

Arrangements were put in hand accordingly, and at the end of June Captain W. J. Jarrard left Penkridge Bank to take command of " E " and " F " Companies, with Captain C. F. Ellwood as second-in-command; while Captain Beley returned to the Service Companies. 2nd Lieut. E. H. P. Pitt left for the Depot about the same time.

On 9th July a Northern Command Order (No. 1228) was published stating that on a locally-raised Battalion moving to its Brigade in the Fourth New Army it would leave its Depot Company or Companies behind, and that the Commanding Officer would cease to have any control over them. The latter clause was subsequently modified to give Commanding Officers the right of approval of suggestions for promotion. Order No. 1228 further specified that Depot Companies of the same regiment would be grouped together, companies of each Battalion, however, remaining separate. For the time being the senior officer was to be placed in command.

In accordance with this Order, the Sheffield Battalion's Depot Companies moved out from Redmires to Silkstone on

Days of Auld Lang Syne. 15

July 23rd, leaving behind at Redmires only a " recruiting party " of twenty-five, under Captain Ellwood. Captain Jarrard took command of the Sheffield and Barnsley reserve companies at Silkstone for the time being, under circumstances of no little difficulty. The last link, as it were, with Redmires was broken on September 6th, when the little " recruiting party " also proceeded to Silkstone.

In the meantime Lieut.-Colonel W. G. Raley, latelv in command of the 14th (S.) Battalion Y. and L. Regiment (2nd Barnsleys) had been appointed to command the 15th (R.) Battalion Y. and L. Regiment, which was formed of the Depot Companies grouped at Silkstone.

Several N.C.O.'s and men of the Battalion were transferred to the Reserves, not by choice, I may state, and some record of the work done by them should be given. " F " Company was wholly formed after the departure of the Battalion from Redmires, and for some considerable time recruits were enlisted for the 12th Battalion, even, in fact, after the Reserves were amalgamated with the 15th (Reserve) Battalion York and Lancaster Regiment.

At the end of December, 1915, Hyde Park Barracks were taken over and used as a recruiting depot for the 12th Battalion, and remained open until April, 1916. The recruits now enlisted afterwards formed the drafts which fed the 12th Battalion in the field. Many of the officers who fought with the Battalion had their training with the Reserves.

On the night of the 25th September, 1915, marching through Ripon in drenching rain, the regiment entrained for the long journey to the South of England, and the following day took over new hutments at Hurdcott Camp, near Wilton, Salisbury.

A few days before, Brigadier-General Bowles had handed over the command of the 94th Brigade to Brigadier-General G. Carter Campbell, D.S.O., late Scottish Rifles, and directly after the arrival in the new camp came a change which affected the Battalion more directly. Colonel C. V. Mainwaring, the Commanding Officer, had for some time been in indifferent health—the result of long service in Eastern climes. The work he did would have been severe for a much younger man, since he always took the very highest view of duty. No one in the Battalion took so little leave.

Just prior to leaving Ripon Camp Colonel Mainwaring was certified unfit for foreign service. Hence it came that on September 28th he gave up the command of the Battalion. It was with sincere regret that the men, returning that day from a route march, learnt that as they had passed him on the road he was leaving them.

The regiment was fortunate to have appointed as Colonel Mainwaring's successor another Regular officer in Lieut.-Colonel J. A. Crosthwaite, late Durham Light Infantry. Colonel Crosthwaite at the time was home on leave from the Front, and brought to the training of the Battalion the latest experiences in the War.

The whole of the time spent on Salisbury Plains was given to rapid preparation for active service. There was a succession of courses of instruction for all ranks. Equipment for all the new-fangled devices of war came to hand in due course, and was put to good use. Leave was cut down to the minimum, and the men worked as perhaps never before.

The only fly in the amber was a sudden descent of the Munitions of War Department upon the regimental preserves with demands for skilled workmen who could make shells and guns, &c. At one time it appeared as though a serious blow would be dealt at the efficiency of the Battalion. But eventually the demands of the Munitions Department lessened and only about fifty men were marked to be taken. Later on it proved possible to excuse a number of these on the ground that they were trained "specialists"—i.e., machine-gunners, transport men, grenadiers, &c.

The Battalion was inspected by Sir A. H. Paget, G.O.C., Salisbury Training Centre; by Major-General Wanless O'Gowan, G.O.C., 31st Division, and by Brigadier-General T. Carter Campbell, D.S.O.

After a certain amount of training in manœuvres the Battalion marched across the Downs one sunny winter's day to Canada Lines, Lark Hill Camp, just vacated by the 91st Brigade. Here they remained from November 16th to

Days of Auld Lang Syne.

November 30th. They received the long-looked-for short rifles, and with each man at last in possession of his own, it was as though a tonic had been administered to the whole regiment. Parts III. and IV. of the General Musketry Course were smartly and keenly completed, and the machine-gun men completed their training in very good style, incidentally taking four of the five prizes put up for inter-brigade competition. In Parts I. and II. the Battalion had made the best record in the 94th Brigade, and in Parts III. and IV. they came out on top.

Chapter Three.
The Early Days Abroad.

*Alexandria   Port Said: Suez Canal: Antics of the Arabs
Pleasant times.*

SOON afterwards the division received sudden orders to prepare for Egypt. Half the Battalion rushed off from Larkhill for a short farewell leave, while the other half marched back to Hurdcott, where leave was cancelled and everyone recalled. There was a hurricane of work and excitement, in which fever and influenza played a part. Eventually the Battalion embarked on December 21st, 1915, on board H.M.T. Nestor (Blue Funnel Line), anchored at Devonport.

The Battalion was at full strength, the officers who also embarked being: Lieut.-Colonel J. A. Crosthwaite, Major T. Carter Clough, V.D., Major A. Plackett, Major A. R. Hoette.

Captains W. A. Colley, D. C. Allen, E. G. G. Woolhouse, R. E. J. Moore, A. N. Cousin, and W. S. Clark.

Lieutenants J. L. Middleton, E. L. Moxey, C. Elam, G. H. J. Ingold, T. L. Ward, C. H. Woodhouse, H. W. Pearson, R. D. Berry, F. W. S. Storry, F. C. Earl, and S. J. Atkinson (Transport Officer).

2nd Lieutenants A. J. Beal, D. E. Grant, J. C. G. Bardsley, C. A. Jackson, F. A. Beal, and J. C. Cowen.

Captain and Adjutant N. L. Tunbridge.

Hon. Lieut. and Quartermaster S. W. Maunder.

Captain G. Mitchell, R.A.M.C.

Captain J. F. Colquhoun, Chaplain.

The departure was a memorable one, for as the ship left the dock the regimental band played "Auld Lang Syne"

The early days abroad. 19

and other appropriate music, and there were constant salutations from the shore, right along to Plymouth Hoe. Small craft on the waters gave cheerful hoots, as everyone took a long last look at England's shores, and, with guardian destroyers on either side, the transport went to sea. Through the billowy Bay of Biscay, the Strait of Gibraltar was reached on the night of Christmas Day. The searchlight from the fortress struck the vessel like a sword. Boxing Day brought with it fair sunshine, lovely skies, and harmonious ripples of the gorgeous Mediterranean. The voyage now became most enjoyable, and with sports and concerts the troops were perfectly content. A brief stay was made at Valetta on December 29th, when the olive-coloured Maltese came in scores in their " bum " boats and youngsters dived continually for coins, dexterously catching them between their toes.

Despite the vagaries of the course owing to the submarine alarms, the Nestor drew up at Alexandria on New Year's Day, 1916, and the notable port provided a splendid picture in the sunlight. In front of the magnificent buildings and mosques, with their eastern colour, were large docks which accommodated all kinds of vessels, from warships and transports to the miniature dhows of the Arabs—a great spectacle.

On the quay side the men had rare fun at the expense of the jabbering natives, who fought among themselves for the odd pence thrown by the troops from the decks and who loudly lamented their treatment by the Egyptian Police, who heartily cuffed them with staves.

After singing farewell to the Nestor the Battalion entrained for Port Said. It was a wearisome journey across the desert in a jolting train, and was of no interest until the dawn, when hundreds of drowsy Arabs emerged from the shelter of little square log huts built alongside the line. At Ismailia were strong bodies of troops, consisting of British, Australians, and Indians, with Camel and Cavalry Corps, and then right along the line to Port Said were troops and camps. The palm trees and giant cacti at the various stations attracted considerable attention. Port Said was reached at 11 a.m., after a journey lasting thirteen and a half hours, and the Battalion encamped behind the town.

20   History of The Sheffield City Battalion.

Port Said is a remarkable town, even though it is called a sink of iniquity. Remarkable, indeed, in the contrasts of every kind. East jostles West, though East predominates. Close to the great railway stations and magnificent buildings are to be seen caravans arriving from or starting for the desert, the grave camels and the noisy locomotives being fully in keeping with the scene of contrasts. Not far away is Arab Town, a mere assemblage of " hutches," erected to the height of innumerable storeys above dark, dirty drinking-shops. All sorts of ugly rumours are associated with Arab Town ; men are drugged with hasheesh in the wineshops and disappear; bodies of over-curious sightseers are discovered in " ginnels " at dawn. The stench, however, is no rumour. If a fire were to start at one end of the town the whole would be destroyed very quickly.

For some unknown reason, visitors to Port Said's Arab Town always think of Sodom and Gomorrah. The natives, who hate water of any description, are rarely handsome, and when they grin the effect is wicked. They always chant when they work; possibly they are calling upon Allah, but invariably it sounds as if they are crying to "Ali, Ali, Baba"! Ten of them accomplish in two hours what one Englishman can do in one. The old water carriers, with skins on their backs, look picturesque at a distance, but close to they become repulsive. In pictures and afar off the flowing robes of the people of the East appear to be superb, but at short range the beauty disappears. One finds that these robes are made of remnants, bits of cloth, which in Britain the housekeeper turns into dusters and patchwork quilts. Men's breeches often are soldiers' pants. Arabs wrap any old thing round their heads and walk about barefooted.

There are several fine buildings in the streets of the European quarter. Each street possesses numerous cafés, which boast minstrel parties from various climes. Amusing, indeed, were the attempts of these alleged musicians to render British popular airs in 1916. The manner in which an Italian girl endeavoured to sing " It's a long, long way to Tipperary " (supported by violinists) was painful and far worse than the melody churned out in the streets of England by the Italian organist on his barrel organ.

Early days at Bramall Lane.

The early days abroad.

Soldiers obtain good lessons in bargaining at Port Said, for they barter with Arabs for souvenirs, and usually bring the price of a fancy brooch from five shillings to one shilling. The shops, including the curiosity shops, are very costly in their goods, and the salesmen ask exceptionally high prices for spears, scarab stones, sword-sticks, and other well-known souvenirs of the East.

The city is always full of gaiety and entertainment. A noteworthy figure is the Egyptian " wizard " in the long flowing robes, who smiles all the time so that you may see his beautiful teeth and calls for his whisky just like " de Inglees." He sits at your tables and performs remarkable feats with three iron cups. You see little chickens come inside the cups and jump on to the tables, jump back, and disappear. The doubling of coins in your clasped hands is comparatively easy. One penny becomes two every time, except in real life.

Port Said is indeed a strange mixture.

For nearly three months the Battalion worked on the defences of the Suez Canal, owing to threats of the Turks at that time.

Truly, the Canal is something more than an Egyptian waterway. It is indeed the Gateway of the East—our ready way to India, China, and Australia. Its total length is about 100 miles, and its width varies from 144 feet to 420 feet, though it passes through what are now five lakes, but what formerly were valleys or depressions. Its depth is now about 31 feet, the bottom being much narrower than the top.

The desert fringes practically the whole course of the Canal. The " half-way house " is Ismailia, a really flourishing town and the headquarters of the Canal officers. In older times it was merely a small Arab village, but now it possesses fine hotels, clubs, restaurants, theatres, and so on. Every vessel in the Canal is controlled from Ismailia.

The Canal has a remarkable history, and is a much older undertaking than is generally known. Rameses II., the ancient Egyptian monarch, originally constructed a waterway connecting the Nile Delta with the Red Sea. In the course of long years the waterway filled up, so that it had been forgotten, save for legend, when it was taken in hand by Darius I. of Persia.

History of The Sheffield City Battalion.

It is impossible to describe fully the hundred and one things concerning the Battalion's life in the East. Enough has been said of Port Said and the Canal, and rough outlines must suffice for the rest. The movements of the Battalion were :—

January 1, 1916—Alexandria.
January 2 to 25—Port Said and Salt Works. (January 6 to 18, " D " Company at Tineh and Ras-el-Esh; January 19 to 25, " B " Company at Tineh and Ras-el-Esh).
January 26 to February 20—El Ferdan.
February 21 to February 22—Kantara.
February 23 to February 26—Hill 80. Off Kantara.
February 27 to March 7—Kantara.
March 8 to March 10—Port Said.

The whole period was more or less a time of training in which the Battalion put theory into practice in the matter of building strong points in the desert, and patrol work on the banks of the Canal. The importance of the business was that the troops were ready at hand if the Turk ventured to seize the waterway. Everyone took the times very seriously, as more than one officer could testify by personal adventure, and good work was done. For instance, the Battalion received special praise for the excellent assistance it gave in laying a Decauville line out to the desert when stationed at El Ferdan.

Each day brought its rumour, and there was a wide range of subjects, too. The Kaiser died several times, and Kut was regularly surrendered by General Townshend. Bulgaria and Austria desired peace every five minutes, while riots in Constantinople were common. The Turks were usually massing in the desert, preparatory to an advance on El Ferdan, Ballah, and Kantara, points which they touched in 1915; and the Battalion was going to sail to France practically every week, though sometimes it might have been India.

In administration naturally there were irksome incidents. At first the men's rations were somewhat poor, and it took nearly all their pay to enliven the monotony of biscuits, bully beef, stew, jam, cheese, and a small portion of bread.

The early days abroad.

At Tineh the men used to get up at 6 a.m. to purchase small Arab cakes from the natives—food seemed so limited.

However, the seamy side was not the only side, and there were many pleasing experiences and sights. Foremost, perhaps, were the antics of the Arabs, to whom a hiding was part of the day's programme. Anything with a blade had a fatal fascination for the Arab. The older it was, the more attractive it was to him. By some means the natives discovered that the Battalion was from wonderful Sheffield, on the other side of the world, and they knew that everything in the blade line came from there. Consequently they haunted the men with awestruck adoration, and if asked what the blazes they wanted, the answer would be, " You give me ' jag-knife '; I give you good Inglees money." A marine-store dealer would make a colossal fortune in the environs of Kantara if he specialized in jaded jack knives—and if he chained them to his person. The Arab is the most happy-go-lucky individual on earth. The only occasion upon which he wears a worried look is when he has been worsted in a bargain.

In physique the Arab is a magnificent specimen, but he disdains toil when it is not for his immediate benefit. His bodily strength is immense, and I have seen an Arab walk on board a dhow, raise upon his shoulders a structure with sufficient space within to billet his wives and family, carry it up a steep bank, plant it down, and start a canteen. On the other hand, a typical scene would be as follows: A gang of ten Arabs were unloading a limber. They were apparently putting forth every ounce of their strength, but the thing did not budge. The unpaid lance-corporal in charge of the party viewed the job with dismay, and the Arabs rolled their eyes and joined together in a dismal lament to Allah. At that moment a grizzled sergeant-major walked up unobserved and snarled out a sentence in Arabic. Throwing one startled glance at him, the toilers abruptly forgot Allah, and, rushing at the limber, sent it bounding over the sand like a toy.

Then there were the adventures with the camel caravans. How could the Arabs prevent camels seizing trousers with their teeth when being loaded up? One of the most amusing sights in the world is to see a camel scrape its foreleg with a hind one. These caravans took stores some eight miles into the desert, where troops were preparing defensive lines.

There were various ships passing through the Canal both day and night. Troopships always provided amusement by the repeated calls, " Who are yer? " On February 6th the Nestor passed, and the vessel was accorded a worthy reception.

Dhows, ancient craft with faded colours and lateen sails were most picturesque.

The growth of the stations on the Canal side was extraordinarily interesting. Immense stores were gradually collected, splendid roads made, and Decauville lines laid. The supply of water was one of the biggest problems. At the time in question water was brought up on barges and emptied into huge tanks on the bank side, but schemes were in progress for laying pipe-lines in various directions. In those days a man shaved and washed in a mugful of water taken from his ration of just over a pint. Happily, there were no restrictions on bathing in the beautiful Canal.

The desert was by no means uninteresting, particularly from the view of the naturalist. In the morning the heavy dews provided pleasing contrasts in colours; while out among the gorse, sand, and palm trees beautiful species of creatures were to be seen. One rarely caught was the kangaroo rat, which burrows through the sands like the wild rabbit on the English common. There were locust, large black and golden beetles, ants, sand-jumpers, snakes, and sand-worms (most delicately marked), and the nervous chameleon. The horrible-looking tarantulas inhabited the bulrushes on the bank of the Canal.

The bleaching bones of camels gleaming in the sunshine reminded one of the historical side of the desert, and the religious students imagined the Children of Israel wandering for forty years and the Queen of Sheba journeying to King Solomon.

The last week at Kantara was devoted to sport, and inter-battalion meetings with Barnsley battalions were keenly contested. Whilst here, numerous families of Armenian

The early days abroad.

refugees arrived, and no one could possibly forget the abject misery of these poor folk as they struggled along with their children and goats.

With the troops coming from Gallipoli and the threat from the Turks evaporating, there was no need for the division to stay in Egypt any longer, and the 12th Battalion embarked at Port Said on March 10th on board H.M.T. Briton.

Before leaving, the Battalion was thanked by the Army Commander for splendid work done on the defences of the Canal.

Chapter Four.
France at last!

> Marseilles: The Heart of France: Incidents of a long journey: Huppy: The Sectors of Colincamps and Hebuterne: Their importance.

THE voyage from Port Said to France occupied five days, the Battalion arriving at Marseilles on the afternoon of March 15th. The trip was a very pleasant one, as the weather was fine practically the whole of the time. There was plenty of sport, and, to add the necessary spice of danger, rumour spoke of impending naval actions by the German Fleet and of the fact that the German Government had offered a reward of £4,000 to the crew of the U-boat successful in sinking the Briton, one of the fastest transports afloat.

As the vessel approached the port, great interest was evinced in the fine rock studies seen ahead. Then appeared the noble cathedral, Ste. Marie Majeure, erected on the site where once stood a temple of Diana and overlooking the harbour of La Joliette. Later one admired the fine châteaux and picturesque villas on the woodland hills of the bay and the magnificent buildings on the lower slopes.

The ship passed through the Gulf of Lyons, and the troops were so keen on noting the striking points of the city and massive harbour, with its wharves, quays, and jetties, that they almost overlooked Cap Martin and the wonderful Château d'If.

One cannot adequately describe the scene or the impressions of those who saw the gradually unfolding picture—wonderful breakwaters; the mass of shipping from all parts of the world; the remarkable suspension bridge; the vast concentrated activity of all; the seamen and dockhands in their rough coloured garb, wearing the gay caps of the Revolution.

The ship anchored at 3 p.m., but the landing was not made until the next morning, when, at 11.30, to the strains of the regimental band, the Battalion marched off from the quay to the entraining point. The strength of the Battalion was: Officers, 30; other ranks, 986.

The decrease of eight other ranks in the number which left England in December was due to sickness in Egypt. With the exception of one, all rejoined the unit at different times later. The exception was No. 12/987 Private H. Marshall (Rotherham), who died in hospital after the Battalion had set sail.

The short march to the railhead was full of interest. First noticed, perhaps, were small groups of German prisoners labouring in the dockyards. They were closely scrutinized as the men stepped light-heartedly by, and the prisoners ceased their work to gaze at the Britons. Most of the captives were well-built men of unprepossessing appearance and very sullen. Maybe the continued sight of the Allies' might being gathered in from all lands chilled their hearts. This passing glimpse was the only sight of the enemy which a good many men of the Battalion obtained, as, later, several were killed and wounded in the deadly monotony of trench warfare without ever coming to close grips with him.

The quaint veteran guards of these aforementioned prisoners aroused much mirth, and many a jest was made at their expense. But through all the pathos was felt, and the sentimental vein was touched when women in odd alleys shed tears; they knew what lay ahead. And maybe some personal loss was keenly felt. Further on, citizens urged themselves into ecstasy of delight as the gallant big drummer twirled his drumsticks to emphasize the beat. To them the man of the moment was the big drummer.

The train, made up of coaches, cattle trucks, and horse-boxes, accommodated over 2,000 troops, in addition to baggage. The Battalion now commenced its memorable journey through the heart of France, and it is interesting to note that within eighteen days of disembarkation the unit had taken over a part of the British Front Line.

As the train slowly moved off round hillsides and over occasional viaducts another magnificent view of the port was obtained. Too soon did the train plunge into the bowels of the mountain. It took twenty minutes to pass through the tunnel, and still the sea was in sight; but this time a different bay was seen. The rolling water on the one hand and mountainous scenery on the other occupied attention. All was delightful. White red-capped cottages and budding verdure lent the land additional colour, and France, indeed, rivalled some of England's proud scenes. Pleasures deepened as the panorama suggested favourite haunts at home. The imposing Lower Alps, with snow-covered tips, some scintillating in the sunshine, some shrouded in mist, were visible for many miles. Later came the plains, the home of the market gardeners of France. Every inch of the ground seemed to be utilized.

Arles, with its Roman splendour, was the first stopping-point, and it also provided the first glimpse of the Rhone. The journey continued; many picturesque towns and villages were passed, noticeable features being the Gallic ruins and splendid avenues of trees. Shortly historical Avignon was reached. Here, as at all other places, the troops met with a cordial reception.

This, of course, is not the place wherein to describe the beauties of Avignon, so many centuries the possession of the Holy See; but reference must be made to the old ruined bridge over the Rhone, the town's ramparts, and, above all, its Papal Palace. The ramparts and the gigantic palace, which was once the fairest and strongest dwelling in the world, were built in the thirteenth century. The English onlooker calls Avignon a combination of York and Conway, and rejoices in the various legends concerning the religious houses, with their belfries and bells, and the gloomy Notre-dame-les-Dome, founded, it is said, in honour of the Virgin, on the site of a temple of Hercules.

Beautifully cultivated land and more castles was the general run of things to the next sojourn—Orange, where pretty Red Cross nurses served out rum and tea, which

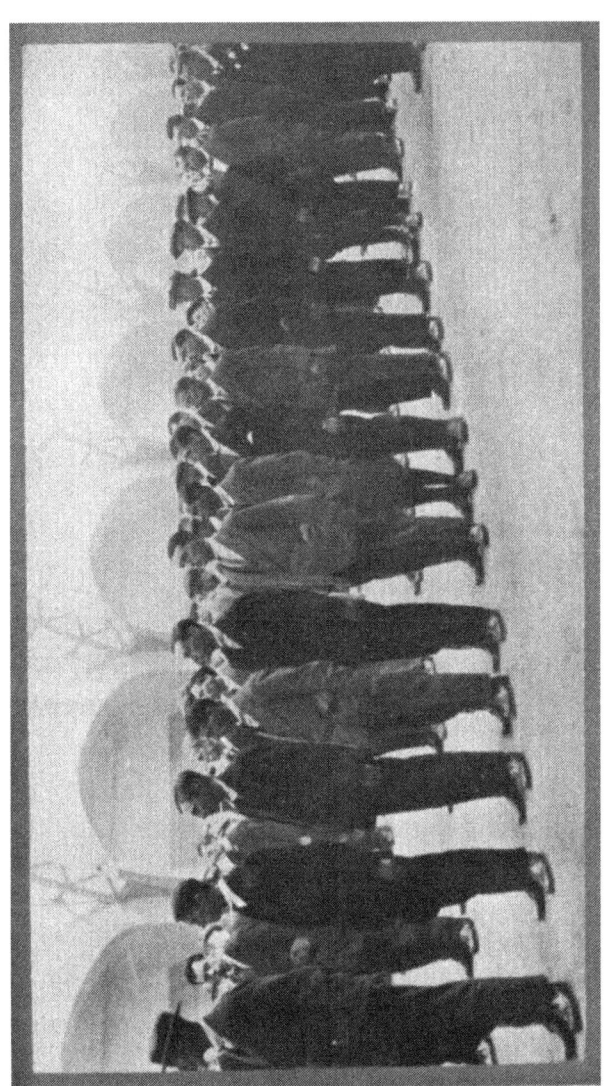

Listening to the late Colonel Hughes' motto: "Work, Work, Work!"

warmed all hearts for the coming night. In the station the hubbub was great, and here the Battalion felt for the first time the Frenchmen's fierce passionate anger against the Germans. The old porters spat, drew their hands across their throats, and plunged imaginary bayonets into the listeners' breasts; the words " Allemand " and " Verdun " pierced the air.

After half an hour the journey recommenced, and then the night. It needs a Dickens to do justice to the interior of one of the horseboxes at this time. A horsebox billeted forty-two men. What need to say more?

Few people troubled about Lyons or any other of the many stations passed through during the night; but there was a general clamouring for tea at 6 a.m., when the train pulled up at Mâcon. Many called, but few were satisfied. Soon all were aboard and off again along the side of the River Saône as far as Châlon; and then to Beaune, of the vines. Pausing on the way to Dijon, a French Red Cross train full of wounded drew up, and many curious conversations followed. One fellow, wishing to see some real fighting Frenchmen, but being crushed out, went to the other side of a horsebox crying, "Aye, lads, there's a waggon-load of men wi'out legs here." He did not gain his object, and, *en passant*, one sorrowfully adds that this jovial chap four months later had his legs riddled almost from off his body by machine-gun bullets in No Man's Land.

Dijon was reached at 12.30 p.m., and Les Laumes, where tea was issued, at 5.0 p.m. The absence of male labour had seemed more conspicuous this day, and the men had waved sympathetically to many an old weather-beaten dame toiling in her white bonnet; also had laughed with the children carrying water from the wells by aid of the yoke. It had been pleasant to see the oxen pulling the plough; the quaint villages in the heart of valleys and on hillsides; the romantic ruins; the statues on lonely hills; the towns and mosaic roofs of the churches.

In the night Tonnerre, Joigny, Sens, Fontainebleau, the fringe of Paris, Versailles were passed through, and by the morning light St. Germain was distinguished. Amiens was reached about noon, and within a short time the detraining point, Pont Remy, situated a few miles south-east of Abbeville. The detrainment was complete by 10 p.m.

The first billet was the old-world village of Huppy, where many pleasing associations were made. Outstanding features of this pretty village were the womenfolk with their white bonnets, the whitewashed cottages with thatched or red-tiled roofs, the long narrow windows, the tall ornamental crucifixes (the little wooden crosses at the foot), the old wells —their log hoods green with age—and the treadmill threshers.

The Battalion stayed there from the night of March 18th to the morning of March 26th, the period being devoted to steady training. It was known that the 31st Division would soon be called upon for duty, and so an early order to move to the line was not unexpected. A four days' march was commenced in a heavy rain on Sunday, March 26th, the Battalion marching to Longpré. The next day the Battalion moved to Vignacourt. On the same day a party of ten officers and forty N.C.O.'s proceeded to the Colincamps sector of trenches for seventy-two hours duty with the 8th (T.F.) Battalion Worcestershire Regiment. They were taken to the Front in motor-'buses via Flixecourt and Doullens, the latter a most important centre of the British Fourth Army at that time.

The party was billeted in Courcelles-au-Bois about midnight, and early the next morning marched to the trenches through the gloomy village of Colincamps. Only occasionally was the sound of firing heard, and little did the officers and men, under the command of Major A. R. Hoette, think that this sector, on the advent of the 31st Division, was to become a perfect hell and the graveyard of hundreds of brave comrades. But of this more anon.

In the meantime 'the regiment had spent the night at Vignacourt, and was on the way to Beauquesne. On March 29th a final halt was made at Bertrancourt. The Battalion encamped in canvas huts, where we will leave it while describing the Colincamps sector, a short length of the Front, wherein the Sheffield "Pals" lived, worked, and died in the cause of Empire and freedom.

France at last! 31

Near the southern extremity of the British Line at that time, from the historic mass of debris known as Hebuterne there stretched to the town of Mailly-Maillet an undulating common called the Colincamps Plain. Midway there stood the village from which it derived its name, and in a slight depression to the East there were the Allied defences—an interminable city with "streets," "lanes," "alleys," "woods," "copses," "avenues," and the like.

Colincamps, situated some two miles from the front line, was representative of Picardy villages—lamentably poor and cheerless. Deserted, save for a roughly-garbed young woman, whose existence appeared to depend upon the number of "œufs" she sold to the troops, the place was a symbol of change and decay. The yellow peasant dwellings of warped beams and baked mud were falling to pieces and the few better-class houses were in a sad way. The church had been battered.

The only place undisturbed for a considerable time was Battalion Headquarters, an oblong schoolroom built of chalk and boasting a slate roof. But this also fell a victim to German bombardment in the end. As a matter of fact, in July, 1918, there was not one stone upon another in the whole village.

In early 1916, troops in Brigade Reserve were generally stationed at Colincamps and accommodated for the most part in barns wherein wire beds had been erected for the comfort of the men.

The objective of all operations on this sector was the village of Serre, which nestled on the other side of the valley and was guarded and fortified with all the ingenious and devilish devices at the command of the enemy. It was a field fort of wonderful strength, and one of the many which marked the German line at this particular time and up to July 1st, 1916. Division after division were led to the assault on Serre's powerful defences, but without success. Constant hammering, however, reduced the place to a pulp, and on the evacuation in February, 1917, it was seen that there was not a square yard of ground untouched by shell. The earth wept in misery and desolation.

Actually, the village faced Hebuterne on the left of the Colincamps sector. The Hebuterne and Colincamps sectors were of great tactical importance, for in a large measure they commanded the valleys and spurs which ran from Hebuterne in the south and south-east directions along which both sides made their lines of defences and in which they both placed their artillery. At the time in question, a very short advance by the enemy against Hebuterne from his lines in Gommecourt Park would not only have enabled him to outflank a large portion of the line to the south and to cut communications leading to the whole of the divisional front, but it would have put out of action all the battery positions, heavy and field, which were situated in large numbers in the Hebuterne-Colincamps Plain. It would also have given the enemy observation over a large area behind the line held by us.

This was, therefore, a very important point of the British defensive line, and was bound to be held at all costs. The enemy spared no pains to secure his hold on the Gommecourt salient, and massed a large number of guns for its defence, which guns were vigorously employed against our lines and Hebuterne and Colincamps. Except on the Hebuterne-Gommecourt Ridge, where the enemy was on equal terms with us, the ground sloped down towards the enemy's lines, which to some extent were commanded by us; but the Rossignol Wood spur and the high-standing village of Serre afforded him good points of observation of our line and thus obviated in a degree the disadvantage of his own inferior position. He was also able to bring a very oblique artillery fire from his position between Gommecourt and Rossignol Wood on any troops attacking from our front.

The position at Hebuterne has been somewhat fully described at this point to enable the reader to realize the position of the Colincamps sector more clearly, and partly because on the Battalion's second visit to the Somme in October, 1916, the Hebuterne portion of the line was taken over and occupied by the 31st Division for over three months.

Chapter Five.
The Baptism of Fire.

The first bombardment: "C" Company's misfortune: The raid of May 16th, 1916: What men did: Billets and training: Wonderful organization: Phases of an attack.

BEFORE the memorable July 1st the Battalion defended the line at Colincamps on four occasions, the periods being—

> April 3rd to 12th.
> May 2nd to 6th.
> May 15th to 20th.
> June 14th to 19th.

In addition, " B " and " D " Companies each acted as support companies to other battalions of the 94th Infantry Brigade.

Compared with what happened afterwards, these periods may now be classed as " quiet times " and merely spells of training in trench warfare; from a battalion standpoint there were several outstanding events which affected both officers and men and created a great impression. There was the first battle casualty; the baptism of fire on the night of April the 6th; the " C " Company misfortune of the 4th of May; the bombardment and raid of the 16th of May; and the traversing of the front line with H.E. shells by the enemy batteries in the Gommecourt salient on the 17th June.

It must not be thought that the above-named were the only occasions on which the men went near the trenches. When the Battalion was out of the line large working parties were continuously provided both day and night for work on trench-digging and for improving communications, &c., and often hard labour was executed under harassing shell and machine-gun fire.

The battle casualties for the months of April, May, and June were as under :—
Officers :—
Wounded: Lieut. C. H. Woodhouse (afterwards rejoined), 2nd Lieut. H. S. Lumb.
Other ranks :—

	C.S.M.s.	Sgts.	Cpls.	L.-Cpls.	Ptes.
Killed	2	2	0	4	25
Died of wounds	0	1	0	1	7
Wounded	0	2	7	5	54
Totals	2	5	7	10	. 86--110

On Sunday, April 2nd, the Battalion marched from Bertrancourt to Colincamps. The move was interesting from two points of view. First, the Battalion was actually on its way to man the trenches, where their long training would be tested, and, secondly, on the previous afternoon Colincamps had been shelled by German " heavies," which searched in vain for two 9.2in. guns in an orchard a little distance from the church. The square church tower received a direct hit, and the Royal Engineers' wooden canteen was swept away. A shell fell in the brigade grenade store without exploding, and another whizzed through the Brigadier-General's bedroom without causing a casualty.

The relief of the 18th Battalion Durham Light Infantry and the 8th Battalion Worcestershire Regiment (T.F.) on April 3rd was completed without any loss, and the front—1,300 yards in length, the right section of the Colincamps sector—was garrisoned. Battalion headquarters were situated in Bow Street, off Cheero Avenue, which was reached via Taupin Avenue and Roman Road, passing Ellis Square on the right!

It is impossible to describe the mixed feelings of everyone on the first night in the line. Men thought of all the gruesome stories " veterans " had told them, and wondered if " Suicide Corner " was such an awful spot as its name suggested. They heard shells piercing the air, and knew not whether they were our own or those of the enemy. Everybody spoke in whispers and peeped " over the lid " with awe,

The Baptism of Fire.

owing to the skill of German snipers. Yet it must be plainly said that all enjoyed the satisfaction of being in the line at last. The spirit was excellent.

The night was very dark and uneventful, though I would not go so far as to say that no sentry mistook as Germans the wooden posts supporting the wire entanglements; or that men did not feel that machine-gunners were firing at them individually as they walked along the trenches. Soon, however, they became accustomed to death-dealing missiles and learnt to gauge the course of a shell or rifle grenade.

The dawn of April 4th was a welcome one, and, with no casualties to report, Major T. Carter Clough, V.D., who was in command of the Battalion owing to the absence of Colonel Crosthwaite on leave, was well pleased. The spell of good fortune was, however, soon broken, for during the morning Private McKenzie, of " D " Company, was killed by a rifle grenade. The news rapidly spread through the battalion, and there was a feeling of sympathy in all. Sincere tribute was paid to this quiet lad, the first of many brave citizens to make the supreme sacrifice in action against the enemy. In the evening he was reverently buried in the little military cemetery in the rear of the line and close to the famous sugar factory called the Sucrerie.

The Sucrerie, for the possession of which the French fought so valiantly in 1915, was merely a blasted heap of ruins, but it was a useful asset in that it was an important water main and had capacious underground accommodation. It was shelled intermittently and was always under observation. The trenches the Battalion occupied were old enemy trenches, and considerable attention was paid to the many telephone wires he had left on the sides and his fine dug-outs. But no one ever imagined the palatial " shelters " the Germans had built beyond No Man's Land.

There was a great deal of very necessary work to be done in the way of deepening communication trenches, connecting up posts, and making the front line continuous; opening up many trenches between front line and support line which had been allowed to fall into disuse, and making more dug-outs for the accommodation of the men. Work was commenced with a will, and at the end of the nine days' tour a vast improvement was noticeable.

The Battalion underwent its first heavy bombardment on the night of April 6th, 1916, and behaved so well that the Corps Commander (Lieut.-General Sir Aylmer Hunter Weston, K.C.B., D.S.O., M.P., VIII. Corps) expressed his " appreciation of the splendid spirit in which the baptism of fire was taken." At 8.0 p.m. the enemy commenced to bombard the British line to the south of the Battalion section, and gradually crept nearer until at 8.55 p.m. a hot fire was being concentrated on the Colincamps sector. Canister bombs, minenwerfer, rifle grenades, all classes of shells were flung on to our line, not so much the actual front line as the support line and a particular spot known as the Redan. The artillery replied to the challenge, and for three hours there was a heavy duel. The gun flashes quivered in the sky for miles, and, combined with the rapid succession of Verey lights and rockets, a remarkable scene was imprinted on the mind.

The troops became greatly excited and the men of one of the front-line companies jumped on to the firestep opening rapid fire on the enemy with huge delight. " Wash out," " Wash out," was yelled repeatedly when enemy shells proved to be " duds " or failed in their object. An old soldier, Sergeant Clay, of "A" Company, provided one of the most amusing incidents. He smelt gas. Donning his anti-gas helmet, he ran along the trench crying " Put yer gas helmets on. They're sending gas shells o'er. Put your helmets on." The sergeant did not realize that one of the eye pieces of his own helmet was broken and, consequently, his helmet rendered useless.

Comparatively speaking, little damage was done to our trenches, and there were no serious casualties.

On April 8th a German minenwerfer, one of the most devastating instruments of death ever invented, fell squarely into one of our posts—No. 10, to be precise—killing two men and wounding seven others. All were of " B " Company, who, under the inter-company relief system, had gone into the front line the previous day. After this it was decided to hold the post with small parties at either end, leaving the centre clear, as this particular point appeared to have been well registered by the enemy.

Marching to the Redmires Camp in 1914.

The Baptism of Fire. 37

On April 9th Lieut. C. H. Woodhouse was slightly wounded, being the first officer casualty. He soon rejoined the Battalion, however, to obtain a reputation for good, conscientious work.

From the last-named date to the day of relief by the 13th (S.) Battalion York and Lancaster Regiment there was nothing but discomfort for everybody. There was a continuous downpour of rain, which could not be effectively drained away in several of the trenches, and all trenches were sludgy and slimy. The nights were cold and the men got soaked to the skin. The nights of the 12th-13th April saw the relief completed and the Battalion encamped in huts on the Bus side of Bertrancourt.

A disturbing event occurred during the Battalion's second period of duty in the line. On May 2nd the Battalion relieved the 14th (S.) Battalion York and Lancaster Regiment in the left section of the sector, and " C " Company was in the left half of the front line. Throughout the next morning there was considerable activity on both sides, and in the afternoon the enemy constantly shelled our positions in and near John Copse—the left of the four copses named after the Gospels. Three wounded men were being attended to when a minenwerfer was hurled into the company telephone dug-out, killing six men, including Company Sergeant-Major J. W. Ellis, and wounding one so badly that he died on the way to the Field Ambulance. Five men were wounded in addition.

Stiff, sturdy, and manly, the sergeant-major was one of the best-liked men in the Battalion, and always was a notable figure. He represented the best type of the British soldier, and the traditions of the British Army were matters of great moment to him. He was also well known in the Hallamshires. A Sheffielder by birth, he joined the 2nd Battalion of the York and Lancasters over a quarter of a century ago, and was in South Africa from 1891 to 1897, serving as a section sergeant with the Mounted Infantry in the Matabele war. In January, 1897, whilst proceeding with the troops to India, he was on the Warren Hastings when she was wrecked. He stayed with the regiment in India until the end of 1898, when he went on the Indian

History of The Sheffield City Battalion.

Volunteer Staff. At the outbreak of the South African war he volunteered for service, and went out with Lumsden's Horse and saw the fighting in and about Johannesburg. Afterwards he stayed on in South Africa with the 14th Battalion Mounted Infantry, with the rank of Sergeant-Major. In 1901 he was specially selected to go to Australia with a number of Colonial troops, returning with a fresh lot of recruits. At the end of the war he returned home, and joined the Battalion in Dover.

From 1904 to 1906 he was sergeant-major of the Mounted Infantry staff in Malta, ultimately rejoining his own regiment with the rank of colour-sergeant. He had four medals—the Matabele 1896, the King's and Queen's South Africa (six bars), and the Long Service Medal. He joined the permanent staff of the Hallamshires in 1909, and held the position of instructor for about two years. He was in civil employment up to the time of the European War.

The trenches continued to be far from comfortable. One post, No. 4, was blown in three times within four days, and Battalion headquarters, at a dug-out called the Monastery, in Monk Trench, were none too safe, as bullets consistently pitched into the trench side near the entrance. "Bloodspuds," the Adjutant called them. A few weeks later this dug-out was destroyed.

On June 6th the Battalion was relieved, and moved to a new rest camp which was being erected in Bois de Warnimont, near Authie. "D" Company, which, it should be here stated, was at this time a permanent working party and had not, in consequence, been doing actual garrison work in the trenches, stayed on at Colincamps. Bois de Warnimont is a place to be remembered. It was a beautiful resting-place for the Battalion after its stress; all men living who made its acquaintance on this day will ever recall the lovely wild flowers and magnificent trees, so tall and proud. It was from this haven that the Battalion marched to the fatal assault of July 1st.

The courage and coolness of the City Battalion was proved on the night of May 15th-16th, when the Germans raided the Hebuterne sector. At 12.30 a.m. the enemy commenced to bombard the line with minenwerfer and shells—

The Baptism of Fire.

77, 10.5 c.m., and 15 c.m.—and simply poured them in on the whole of the Hebuterne sector's fire trenches and some of the communication trenches. So intense was the bombardment that some of the trenches were quite obliterated, while others were reduced to a deplorable state. The wire in many places was completely shot away. There was no cessation of the bombardment until 2.45 a.m.

At 1.0 a.m. a party of Germans was seen in the front trenches, and, as the hostile fire lifted a little, a bombing party was formed to bomb them out. After some fifteen minutes' fighting the raiders were driven out, suffering heavy casualties. Other Germans, however, had passed between the front line and support line, coming in on the front-line posts from the rear. On one of the posts most of the rifles had been smashed by direct hits. The lance-corporal in charge fearlessly attacked a German officer with his fists, but it cost him his life. On two other isolated posts no one could afterwards be found, and it was presumed the men had been buried. Some of the Germans wore khaki, with white armlets.

The 12th had practically completed the relief of the 18th Battalion West Yorkshire Regiment when the trouble began. "C" Company was in the left half of the Battalion front line and "B" Company in the right half, their respective commanders being Captain (then 2nd Lieut.) D. E. Grant and Captain (then Lieut.) J. L. Middleton. These young officers, who were only in command temporarily, performed their duties with marked ability under disconcerting circumstances.

The terrific barrage of the enemy was not solely confined to the Hebuterne sector. To cover his actual operations and to create uncertainty he placed a curtain of fire on the Battalion front, and in achieving his object inflicted considerable casualties on us. When it was reported by the battalion on the left that the Germans had succeeded in getting into our lines, guards were rushed up to each of the entrances to the Colincamps sector, and these were reinforced by servants and runners.

Writing about the bombardment a few hours later Captain Grant said:

> I was not disturbed about the " X " retiring. I felt confident the Boche could not get in to my line. I went along my line and found everything in order to ward off an attack. I stopped for a while at No. 12 post and observed the fire. A continual rain of H.E. and shrapnel was falling in No. 11 post, and the line of the barrage was at that time from No. 11, behind No. 12 to Rob Roy, where it joined Nairne, and then to our left front.
>
> I asked for a couple of volunteers from each of the posts, 14, 13, and 12, to help to dig out the dead in No. 11 post. After I left, a number of the sappers in the mine gave efficient help. I went back along the line and along Nairne to Rob Roy to find out the extent of the damage. The men stood to until dawn, when we removed the casualties. Rations were buried, but we salvaged them all. The men behaved splendidly, and showed fine spirit.

The trenches chiefly damaged were Excema, in the vicinity of Observation Wood, Le Câteau, Rob Roy near the junction with Nairne, and Nairne to front line. The front line was levelled in places, particularly near Luke Copse. The Battalion casualties amounted to fifteen killed and forty-six wounded, all men of the ranks. Of course, it is impossible to mention the valour of everyone, but the exceptional devotion to duty of some of the brave fellows deserves mention.

One incident is best described in the clear and circumstantial account of the late Pte. Leonard McIver, who wrote to Dr. R. H. Mathews concerning the death of Pte. R. H. B. Mathews. McIver wrote:

" It was my first time in the trenches, and Mathews took me in hand and gave me cheery advice, promising to keep an eye on me and answer any questions. Later, when the bombardment commenced, he got me at his side. The parapet was blown in and buried me completely, but I found that I was getting air through a small hole, and so called for help. Mathews was surprised to find I was alive, I

The Baptism of Fire.

think, and set about to try and extricate me. He found the weight too great, so discovered my air-hole and scraped at it for some time. This gave me more scope for breathing. To this act I think I owe my life. The hole supplied me with air for about an hour and a half, when a working party found me on hearing me call.

"While your son was clearing out the hole his hand found mine, and, with a strong grip on it, he assured me that he would get me out somehow. At this moment I heard a loud bang, and the hand went limp in mine. I cannot express how sorry I am at being the cause of this sad accident, but, believe me, I shall always think with gratitude of my one-time comrade and his noble sacrifice on my behalf."

12/742 **Pte. R. T. Owen.**—Although wounded in the hands and face, this soldier continued to use his rifle until it became so clogged with his blood that it would no longer work.

12/825 **Pte. R. Wilson.**—Wounded in the back somewhat severely, Pte. Wilson lay in the bottom of the trench filling clips with loose ammunition until evacuated by stretcher-bearers.

12/822 **Pte. B. C. Wilkinson,** 12/785 **Pte. E. Spencer.**—These two men brought up fresh supplies of S.A.A. from Company Reserve in Rob Roy when that trench and Nairne communication trench were being heavily shelled. They had to climb out of the trench in several places where it was blown in, and in doing so Pte. Wilkinson was stunned for several minutes by shrapnel hitting his helmet. They persevered, however, and were successful in their attempt to bring up ammunition.

12/1358 **Pte. G. Hanson.**—After being extricated with difficulty from a dug-out in which he had been buried with others, he displayed exceptional coolness, lighting a cigarette and immediately assisting to dig out the remaining men under heavy shell fire.

12/392 **Corpl. M. C. P. Headeach.**—This N.C.O., though blown off his feet repeatedly by concussion, visited

History of The Sheffield City Battalion.

several destroyed posts on the right of the Battalion line during the bombardment. He showed splendid coolness in aiding the wounded and removing the dead.

12/548 **Lce.-Cpl. F. E. Watkins.**—Lce.-Cpl. Watkins remained at his post when all his men were killed or wounded until ordered to leave it by Cpl. Headeach. Several times he was thrown to the ground.

The undermentioned dug out several comrades despite the falling shells:

2nd Lieut. J. Thompson.
12/755 Sgt. B. J. Register, killed whilst at work.
12/628 Sgt. H. C. Crozier.
12/1069 Sgt. W. Thompson.
12/851 Pte. F. O. Appleby.
12/744 Pte. J. O. Schofield.
12/758 Pte. F. O. Rideout.
12/615 Pte. N. W. G. Chandler.
12/608 Pte. S. Brown.
12/747 Pte. F. J. Pennington.

Cpl. J. H. Marsden also rendered very distinguished services.

Of the above Sgt. Crozier, Lce.-Cpl. Watkins, Pte. Wilson, Pte. Wilkinson, Pte. Spencer, Pte. Hanson, Cpl. Headeach received the Military Medal as a reward for their gallant conduct.

It is pathetic to note that nearly all those just mentioned died on July 1st.

The 16th May was quiet, but there were two or three additional casualties. One was a particularly sad case. A young draft soldier of " D " Company, for some unknown reason, proceeded to the trenches with the Battalion instead of staying with two platoons (working party) of the Company billeted at Colincamps. On the night of the 16th a shell burst over him and killed him while he was assisting to convey the bodies of slain comrades to the cemetery.

The 17th, 18th, and 19th May passed without further momentous happenings, but at this period it became apparent that the British had achieved superiority in aircraft. British aviators were constantly reconnoitring enemy territory, taking photographs, noting new trench work, and spotting battery positions. The bravery of these intrepid airmen as

The Baptism of Fire. 43

they flouted the hostile anti-aircraft gunners called forth general admiration. Over 200 shots were noted as having burst round one aviator alone on 19th May.

The 11th Battalion East Lancashire Regiment relieved the Battalion on the 20th, and billets at Courcelles-au-Bois were taken over. The two platoons of " D " Company continued to stay at Colincamps.

There were stirring times when the Battalion defended the divisional sector in June. The game was afoot, and the enemy knew it. In spite of precautions it was impossible to hide from him all traces of the enormous preparations which were being made for the coming offensive. His observation balloons naturally noted the increased activity behind the line and the large working parties which never ceased their labours; also it was impossible always to drive back his airmen before they had taken photographs—which showed accurately new trench work completed and in progress.

His battery positions and lines of communication testified to the growing volume of British gun-fire. He was fidgety. He was disturbed at the relentlessness of his opponents and the silent thoroughness of their work on a long front. He knew not when the actual blow would fall. At varying times he dropped heavy concentrated fire on the line and harassed back areas, displaying considerable nervousness.

As soon as the relief of the 10th Battalion East Yorkshire Regiment had been completed, the Battalion commenced deepening and repairing the trenches, and, with the enemy in such a nervous state of mind, the men were kept exceedingly busy. On the 15th June Le Câteau and Rob Roy trenches were knocked in in parts, and the next day Le Câteau was again badly damaged.

On the 17th, from 8.30 a.m. to 5.30 p.m., enemy heavy batteries shelled the front line consistently with high explosives, and created havoc with it and the traffic trench. Company-Sergeant-Major W. Marsden, of "A" Company, one of the old soldiers who had joined the Battalion on its formation and had done much valuable work, was killed in his dug-out in the afternoon whilst sleeping. One H.E.

shell landed on top of the dug-out at Post 35, and before the sergeant-major could escape three more fell in exactly the same spot, wrecking the place entirely. Volunteers soon endeavoured to dig him out, despite 77mm. shells and rifle grenades, but, after many hours of laborious work, the attempt had to be given up.

"A" Company also received another blow the same day, Sergeant Clay being killed whilst touring the front line.

At 1.40 a.m. on the night of 17th-18th June the enemy blew up a land mine at John Tunnel (afterwards " sap "), causing casualties.

The 19th June saw more heavy shelling on the same positions as on the 17th. Our artillery retaliated, but did not succeed in silencing the enemy until 3 p.m., at which hour the Battalion commenced to be relieved by the East Lancashires. This day's casualties included 2nd Lieut. H. S. Lumb, who joined the Battalion for duty on 23rd April. "A" Company suffered chiefly.

Altogether, this time four men had been killed and twenty-one wounded, twelve of the wounded cases being "Shell shock." Many people are inclined to smile at the term "Shell shock," but often they do sufferers a great injustice. For instance, one of the shell shock cases was an unfortunate man who had been driven insane by concussion. Seizing a tin of jam, this soldier juggled with it perpetually and refused to part with it. Occasionally he vowed it was a German bomb. Some victims lost all sense of hearing and faculty of speech.

It is worth recording that at this time the trenches were outlined with gay flowers—brilliant poppies, charlock, blue cornflowers, and scabious—and many wondered what truth resided in the very deep-rooted belief that the blood of the slain affects the colour of the flowers, and that special flowers spring up to commemorate special deeds.

It is now advisable to look upon two other phases of the Battalion life during the months April, May, and June—
       (1) Training for Offensive Action;
       (2) Working Parties;
but before proceeding directly to deal with these phases a few broad outlines of billet life in France would perhaps be of interest.

On the march—Old Familiar Faces!

The Baptism of Fire.   45

The billeting area allotted to the 31st Division centred on Bus-les-Artois and its boundaries. It had experienced war's alarms like every place in Northern France. During the retreat of Napoleon Bonaparte, and at the time of his abdication in 1814, the district was occupied by Cossacks, who incessantly clamoured for "Cognac, Cognac"—the only French they knew. In the Franco-German war of 1870-1 the villages, after the battle of Bapaume, were overrun by companies of the Bavarian Infantry, and in August, 1914, the Germans passed through. In June, 1915, the French Divisional Staff temporarily took up their residence at Courcelles-au-Bois whilst directing the advance movement in the direction of Hebuterne. All the villages at one time or another were shelled by the enemy, and all bore the scars of war. At Courcelles, while the Battalion was billeted there, there lived an old lady, the daughter of one of Napoleon's Grenadiers who took part in the battle of Waterloo.

The principal industry appeared to have been agriculture, and this fact probably was responsible for a certain uncouthness and lack of progressive spirit on the part of the people in this area.

Billets usually were either hutments or barns, and both, in varying degrees, were as comfortable as weather and porous dwellings permitted. If the weather was fine, all was bright. If not, it was a matter of dodging raindrops and avoiding pools. There were no complaints about insufficient ventilation. Feather beds, of course, were left in England; but the substitutes—straw, wire-beds, and Mother Earth—always provided a restful couch for the tired body. Give a soldier a blanket and a great coat and he will sleep on blocks of stone as soundly as on flocks and cushions.

Is there any need to dwell on the uses of the soldier's "billy-can"—wash-bowl, teapot, stewpot, shaving-pot?

One of the greatest troubles was the plague of lice. The authorities did their best to combat this evil, but it was impossible for the men to keep clean for many days together. Lice preyed on the minds of some men to such an extent that they dreamed of vermin as big as Bermuda centipedes crawling over them.

One pleasant and redeeming feature was the relaxation in the evenings (when there were no working parties), estaminets, canteens, and Y.M.C.A. huts each providing enjoyment and rest.

The training of troops for offensive action was at this time in full progress, and few people in the United Kingdom realized the greatness of the work nor its importance. It was almost a colossal task for the High Authorities, and called for perfect organization, tutorship, and discipline.

At General Headquarters there was a school for the training of officers for staff appointments; another for advanced teaching of machine gun work to officers and men of machine-gun companies; a third for the benefit of musketry instructors. A Lewis Gun School was established for the instruction of both officers and men. Officers' classes were chiefly devoted to organization and tactical subjects, but the men were well trained in the mechanical side of the Lewis gun, and enabled to realize the properties and limitations of the weapon. There were schools for the teaching of bridging, wireless telegraphy, transport duties, all kinds of field engineering; and then came the Army schools. All the armies, corps, divisions, brigades had their schools, wherein all phases of fighting were taught. The result was that the line units were able to have a continual supply of efficient instructors in the various branches of Army activity. The instructors on their return to the units imparted their knowledge to company officers and N.C.O.'s, so that every individual in the end was taught the latest development in his particular employment. The British armies were trained as they fought. There were attack rehearsals by divisions, brigades, and battalions over land in rest areas.

Chapter Six.
Eve of the Somme Battle.

> Working Parties: Visit of Commander-in-Chief: Final preparations for July 1st, 1916: Duty of the 31st Division: Complaints of the individual enemy.

AND now we pass on to working parties. There was no such thing as the old "fatigue parties," and the man who performed the duties of carrying, digging, &c., to the utmost of his ability was counted (and quite rightly, too) as having done as much to defeat the enemy as the man who went on patrol or took part in an attack.

The first of the five phases of an attack was "the organization of our trenches for the assembly of the attacking force," and this meant defensive work as well as new work in construction. There was the never-ceasing duty of keeping trenches, entanglements, dug-outs, &c., in a proper state of repair and sanitation. An additional holdfast to a revetment or a few minutes pumping every morning would probably save a whole fire-bay or dug-out from collapsing.

The 31st Division commenced its organization of trenches immediately on arrival in the area, and the Sheffield and Barnsley Battalions played their part so well in this direction that there was always a great demand and a world of praise for "The York and Lancaster Working Parties." As previously mentioned, "D" Company, under Major Hoette, was a permanent working party from May 2nd to May 16th, and two platoons until the end of the month. The splendid work this Company did drew forth the following commendation:

"H.Q., 94th Infantry Brigade.

"I desire to bring to your notice the keenness and industry shown by the Permanent Working Party of the 12th York and Lancaster Regiment during the past fortnight.

"(Sgd.)   G. J. P. GOODWIN, Major R.E.,
"O.C. 223 Field Company."

The Brigadier-General G. T. C. Carter-Campbell, D.S.O., commanding the 94th Infantry Brigade, informed the Commanding Officer (Lieut.-Col. Crosthwaite) of his pleasure on receiving such a good report of the work done by the Battalion.

Further honour was gained for the Battalion by Captain (then 2nd Lieut.) T. E. Grant, who, being appointed Brigade Pioneer Officer on May 2nd, showed so much zeal, enterprise, and fearlessness in superintending trench work that he was mentioned in dispatches by the Commander-in-Chief.

The work chiefly consisted of repairs to damaged trenches, the opening up of neglected ones, and the digging of assembly and communication trenches. One or two communication trenches were converted into fire trenches. But quite early much road work had to be done in the district owing to the heavy rains and traffic. Before the "push" considerable attention was paid to the wire defences, and carrying parties were a daily and nightly feature. There appeared to be a never-ending stream of ammunition, bombs, grenades, rockets, lights, and Stokes' T.M. bombs between Colincamps and the front line. A week before the attack huge gas cylinders were emplaced in the line.

The tasks were neither pleasant nor safe, and the officers as well as men often had to endure hardships. The Battalion's first experience in this sphere of labour almost broke all hearts, and folk who had called distasteful events "pin pricks" now said "sword thrusts" instead.

On two or three occasions there were casualties in the working parties. On May 1st a party under Lieut. Ingold and Lieut. Storry was shelled at Ellis Square, one man being

Eve of the Somme Battle. 49

killed and three others wounded. On the 29th of the same month " D " Company's wirers came under machine-gun fire, one man being killed and two wounded. It was remarkable that more casualties did not occur.

On May 10th, while the Battalion was resting at Warnimont Wood, Field-Marshal Earl Haig visited the area and watched the Battalion as it carried out " refresher " training. The day of the visit was a beautiful one, and the approach through the wood of the Commander-in-Chief with his brilliant cavalcade of staff officers, Lancers, and Guards was noble and inspiring. It was but a glimpse of a world's great man, but a glimpse never to be forgotten.

Major-General R. Wanless O'Gowan, C.B., commanding the division, inspected the Battalion on June 1st and complimented the men on their excellent conduct on the nights of May 15th and 16th. " There's a lot of work to be done," he said, " and you will be to the front when the great offensive commences."

The next interesting event was the Battalion's practice of communication with aircraft in operations. This took place on 3rd June, at Bus, and was very noteworthy, being a practical test of the theory of inter-communication between infantry and aircraft.

On June 5th, the Battalion marched to Gezaincourt to practice the assault with the remaining brigade battalions. A week was spent in this village, and it was one of the happiest times ever spent in France by the Battalion. Gezaincourt, situated in the heart of a lovely valley, was close to Doullens, a great attraction from all points of view. The day's labour ended, the men flocked to Doullens, the first fair-sized town they had ever seen since their arrival on the miserable, ruined Somme, and " made hay while the sun shone." They were as youths to whom the evil day had come not.

It was at this point that Major Clough was evacuated to the base, and thence to England, with a serious knee trouble. The Battalion was sorry to lose the genial Second-in-Command, for he had been associated with it since the commencement, and had done much valuable work, particularly in administrative directions. He was always

E

sympathetic towards the men, and he was a man of Sheffield. In tabulated form I give the moves of the Battalion from the time of arrival in France to the end of June:

1916.	Destination.
March	15—Marseilles.
,,	18—Huppy.
,,	26—Longpré.
,,	27—Vignacourt.
,,	28—Beauquesne.
,,	29—Bertrancourt.
April	2—Colincamps.
,,	3—Line.
,,	12—Bertrancourt.
,,	28—Colincamps.
May	2—Line.
,,	6—Bois de Warnimont.
,,	15—Line.
,,	20—Courcelles-au-Bois.
,,	30—Bus Wood.
June	5—Gezaincourt.
,,	13—Bus.
,,	14—Line.
,,	19—Bois de Warnimont.
,,	30—Line.

Officers who joined the Battalion were: 2nd Lieuts. C. C. Cloud, P. K. Perkin, E. M. Carr, E. N. M. Butterworth, J. Thompson, H. S. Lumb, Lieut. H. Oxley, 2nd Lieuts. C. H. Wardill, W. H. Rowlands, F. Dinsdale.

The preceding pages, though devoted to the doings of a single battalion, show how methodically, thoroughly, and relentlessly the British prepared for the tremendous assault on the Somme. The blow about to be struck was to shake the enemy as he had never been shaken before, and to make him realize—probably for the first time—that the British land power was no longer to be treated with contempt, but treated as a most serious menace.

The Somme offensive had been planned for some months, but the hour at which the stroke should be made was not known until the year had well advanced. It depended upon the Verdun battle.

Eve of the Somme Battle.

The French, in order to permit of the British Commander training and developing his citizen armies, hung on to the Verdun defences until their strength was almost on the breaking-point. True, they had inflicted enormous casualties on the enemy in this grim, prolonged struggle; but they, too, had lost heavily. And there seemed to be no ending to the German reinforcements and no limit to his madness to secure Verdun. He counted not the cost.

In the early days of June, Marshal Joffre asked for relief. That relief was forthcoming. The British offensive was timed to commence on June 29th, the hour 7.30 a.m.

In the forward area huge dumps of ammunition, equipment, and stores for every arm of the Service were rapidly formed. Wonderful transport work was performed. Day and night thousands of troops conveyed S.A.A., Stokes' mortar shells, "football" bombs, hand grenades and rifle grenades, rations and water to selected points in the trenches. Hundreds of gas cylinders were installed in the front line by carrying-parties and special brigades. Supplies never failed in a single direction. Indeed, the organization was well-nigh perfect.

The duty of the 31st Division in the great offensive was to form a defensive flank for the remainder of the Fourth Army, which was to attack the German first-line system. In order to be in a position to form this flank the division had first to capture the village of Serre, and the taking of the village was considered essential to the success of the general operation. It was the duty of the 94th Infantry Brigade to carry this operation to a successful conclusion.

The attack of the 31st Division was to be carried out by two brigades—the 93rd on the right and the 94th Brigade on the left. The 92nd Brigade, less one company, was in divisional reserve.

The frontage occupied by the 94th Brigade was approximately to be 700 yards, extending from John Copse to the southern point of Matthew Copse, and this was to be shared by the 11th (S.) Battalion East Lancashire Regiment and the 12th (S.) Battalion York and Lancaster Regiment, the former on the right and the latter on the left, the post of honour. Each battalion was to have an approximate frontage of 350 yards. The 13th and 14th Battalions York and Lancaster Regiment were to be in brigade reserve, 13th York and Lancaster Regiment on the right and 14th Battalion York and Lancaster Regiment on the left.

June 24th was described as " U " day, and the preliminary bombardment opened, the artillery commencing to cut the German wire.

June 25th was " V " day, and the heavy artillery bombardment commenced. On the VIIIth Corps front three German observation balloons were destroyed on the afternoon by bombs from our aeroplanes.

June 26th was " W " day. In the early evening Major-General R. Wanless O'Gowan, C.B., spoke to the assaulting troops of the Battalion:

" The local German reserves have already come up owing to the bombardment," he said; " but, unfortunately for them, they have run into a lot of deadly gas, which we have been letting off on the Fourth Army front. Never before have we had such a preponderance in all arms as now. We have superiority in numbers also. The village of Serre will be taken."

June 27th was " X " day, and the gathering guns increased their roarings and aviators became exceedingly venturesome and annoying to the enemy. At every available opportunity there were discharges of gas and smoke along the whole line, and the enemy was severely punished.

Raiding and wire-examining parties were sent out every night and Bangalore torpedoes were taken in order to cut wire. Several men of the Sheffield Battalion showed bravery and coolness whilst on this work, and the undermentioned were mentioned for valour on the night June 27th-28th, when hostile artillery and trench mortars were particularly active:

Lieut. F. W. S. Storry (mentioned in dispatches).
*Sgt. R. Henderson.
Lce.-Cpl. G. W. Jones.
Pte. A. K. Rigg.
Pte. G. F. Wagstaffe.
Pte. J. S. Swift.
Pte. J. H. Kelk.

* Died of wounds.

The Civic Farewell at the Town Hall, May 13th, 1915.

Eve of the Somme Battle.

*Pte. H. Storey.
Lce.-Cpl. A. Rixham.
*Pte. T. E. Gambles.

* Died of wounds.

June 28th was " Y " day; but in the afternoon the order came that operations had been postponed forty-eight hours owing to the heavy rains; the trenches were in many places half-full of water, and enemy retaliation at certain points had badly damaged our line.

So far as the divisional front was concerned, blown-in parts of the front line and communications had been repaired, but Rob Roy trench, which it was hoped to use as an assembly trench, was so badly knocked about and so thoroughly registered by enemy batteries that the idea had to be abandoned. There was still a good deal of water to be drained away.

The terrific bombardment and general aggressiveness continued. Writing about the gun-fire, a German soldier said:—

At the first two shots that fell near us I shook all over and lay like one paralysed, and prayed that I might be released from this hell.

Another wrote in his diary thus:

The war fanatics and their friends ought to go through this literal hell and feel its effects on their own bodies, and then they themselves would surely come to the decision: Peace, peace at any price, is the only maxim that ought to direct the Government's policy.

An unknown German soldier spoke of British gas attacks as follows:

An unparalleled slaughter has been going on. Not a day passes but the English let off their gas waves over our trenches at one place or another. I'll give you only one instance of the effects of this gas—people 7-8 kilometres behind the front have become unconscious from the tail-end of the gas clouds. Its effects are felt even 12 kilometres behind the front. One has only to look at the rifles after a gas attack to see what deadly stuff it is.

They are red with rust, as if they had lain for weeks in the mud. And the effect of the continuous bombardment is indescribable.

Our Air Service made a great impression, too. The following is an extract from a captured German document:

Just a word about our own aeroplanes. Really, one must be almost too ashamed to write about them; it is simply scandalous. They fly up to this village, but no further; whereas the English are always flying over our lines directing artillery shoots, thereby getting all their shells, even those of heavy calibre, right into our trenches. Our artillery can only shoot by the map, as they have no observation. I wonder if they have any idea where the enemy's line is, or ever even hit it. It was just the same at Lille. There they were sitting in the theatre covered with medals, but never to be seen in the air.

A further extract:

You have to stay in your hole all day, and must not stand up in the trench, because there is always a crowd of English over us. Always hiding from aircraft, always with about eight or ten English machines overhead; but no one sees any of ours. Our airmen are a rotten lot.

Such were the complaints of the individual enemy.

Chapter Seven.
The Gallant Fight for Serre.

The momentous day: Historical telegrams: The battle by minutes: The spirit of the men: "B" Company's heroism: Thrilling deeds: "A band of heroes": Many tributes: The casualties.

I GIVE as full an account as possible of the momentous day, July 1st, 1916. June 30th—Now the second " Y " day opened sadly. It was seen that the commanding officer (Lieut.-Col. Crosthwaite) was seriously ill, and Major Plackett was hurriedly recalled from the Divisional School, where he had been commandant, to assume command. The gallant colonel, who had shown such contempt for danger, was suffering from the effects of batterings received at Ypres in the early stages of the war, and had to be taken to hospital. Painful and bitter indeed did he find the parting, for he was proud of his splendid Battalion—" his boys."

The first intimation the troops had that all was not well was at 11 a.m., when Major Plackett took command of a battalion parade drawn up for an address by the corps commander. The corps commander, Sir Aylmer Hunter Weston, made a rousing speech. He spoke swiftly and confidently of the advance to be made on the morrow, but emphasized the importance and difficulties of the task allotted to the Sheffield Battalion. The chances of success were exceedingly great, for the British had superiority in numbers, in artillery, in every arm, and in equipment. The Battalion was fighting for the highest of ideals—for the defence of home and Empire.

" But your lot is a very heavy one, and a huge responsibility is shared equally by every individual. No individual

56 History of The Sheffield City Battalion.

soldier may say he has no responsibility. The 29th Division, on your left, performed glorious feats of arms at Gallipoli; the 4th Division, on the right, did wonders in the great retreat from Mons. The feats of these divisions will never be forgotten as long as the world endures. You are Englishmen, even as they, and now you have your opportunity to shine. You will have to stick it. You MUST stick it. I salute each officer, N.C.O., and man."

At 3 p.m. the following message was received from the 94th Infantry Brigade:

To-morrow, July 1st, will be " Z " day. Zero will be 7.30 a.m.—94 Inf. Bde.

Brigadier-General H. C. Rees, D.S.O., issued the following Special Order of the Day:

Brigade H.Q.

You are about to attack the enemy with far greater numbers than he can oppose to you, supported by a huge number of guns.

Englishmen have always proved better than the Germans when the odds were heavily against them. It is now OUR opportunity.

You are about to fight in one of the greatest battles in the world, and in the most just cause.

Remember that the British Empire will anxiously watch your every move, and that the honour of the North Country rests in your hands.

Keep your heads, do your duty, and you will utterly defeat the enemy.

(Signed) F. S. G. PIGGOTT, Captain,
Brigade Major, 94th Infantry Bde.

At 7 p.m. the assaulting troops moved off from Warnimont Wood to march to the assembly trenches behind John Copse and Mark Copse. No music as they slowly wended their way down the woodland side. All faces expressed determination. A lump rises in the throat. What were the thoughts of these wonderful soldiers, who kept their anxieties to themselves? I can do no better than quote the thoughts of two noble sons of the Battalion who were to die next day:

The Gallant Fight for Serre.

*SHADOW.

O, why should Youth, whose symbol is the lark
   That mounts with new-born dreams into the sky,
   Be doomed at frequent intervals to lie
Voiceless and dreamless, prostrate in the dark?
Why, 'mid the laughter of the carnival,
   The feast of roses sensuous with delight,
Why should there break the terror of a call,
   Death calling Youth into the unknown night?
For thus at morn the twilight-footed Death
   Sweeps from the Zenith to the orient rim
Where Youth doth play; and soon his phantom wreath
   Fadeth like beauty into distance dim;
Fadeth like yon rich sunset in the sky
That seems, O sad and tenderly, to die.

CHALLENGE.

Go tell yon shadow stalking 'neath the trees
   With silent-footed terror, go tell Death
He cannot with life's vast uncertainties
   Affright the heart of Youth. For Youth cometh
With flush of impulse, passion to defeat,
   Undaunted purpose, vision clear descried,
To counteract, lay at Death's unseen feet
   The gauntlet of defiance. Far and wide,
Beyond the fear of that unknown exile,
   That brim of time, that web of darkness drawn
Across Life's orient sky, there breaks a smile
   Of light that swells into the hope of dawn:
A dream within the dark, like evening cool,
Like sunset mirror'd in yon darken'd pool.

---

* Reproduced from Sergeant J W. Streets' "The Undying Splendour" by kir permission of Mr. Erskine Macdonald.

History of The Sheffield City Battalion.

TRIUMPH.

Thus dreaming in the shadows of the pines,
  Feeling the presage of the unborn years,
I know that Youth will brave the dark confines
  And wrest from Death his diadem of fears.
I know that should I still and prostrate lie
  Amid Death's harvest there on France's plain
No false regret shall scorning wander by
  And taunt me that my Youth hath been in vain.
Rather in my last moments will I live
  My life's past purpose rich in destiny,
Its scorn of ease, its eagerness to give
  Challenge to all blind to eternity.
Death will not, cannot wrest from out my mind
The thought that Love its life in death can find.

        (By the late JOHN W. STREETS,
      Sgt., 12th Service Bn. York and Lancs. Regt.)

*LINES BEFORE GOING.

Soon is the night of our faring to regions **unknown**,
There not to flinch at the challenge suddenly **thrown**
By the great process of Being—daily to see
The utmost that life has of horror, and yet to be
Calm and the masters of fear. Aware that the soul
Lives as a part and alone for the weal of the whole,
So shall the mind be free from the pain of regret,
Vain and enfeebling, firm in each venture, and yet
Brave not as those who despair, but keen to maintain,
Though not assured, hope in beneficent pain,
Hope that the truth of the world is not what appears,
Hope in the triumph of man for the price of his tears.

      (By the late ALEXANDER ROBERTSON,
     Cpl., 12th Service Bn. York and Lancs. Regt.)

   *Reproduced from Alexander Robertson's "Comrades" by kind permission of
        Mr. Elkin Mathews.

The Gallant Fight for Serre.   59

The 1st of July, 1916, will be remembered as one of the saddest and most tragic, yet withal one of the most glorious, pages of Sheffield history, for on that day there fell in battle the largest number of Sheffield men ever known. Around it sacred memories will ever cling as citizens recall the gallant men who in a few minutes put to the test their long months of training.

"July 1st" will be indelible words in every Englishman's mind and keywords to almost incomprehensible thoughts and scenes. The man who was present at the battle for Serre will at their mention see again the day before the battle—the toilsome journey through the trenches, half-full of water; see again the tired slumberers of the dawn, the beautiful summer morn, the faultless parade on the parapets, and the unwavering quick march into the hail of bullets and shells; see again those brave comrades mowed down as grass before the scythe, and those odd parties crossing the German trenches, alas! never to return.

He will again see the lightning shell-bursts, hear their stunning crashes and feel the shakings of tortured earth. He will recall the mangled, blackened bodies and hear the groans of ghastly wounded and voices of grey-faced soldiers as they said to themselves, "Let us hush this cry of 'Forward' till one thousand years have gone."

And as his thoughts travel he will clench his fists at the recollections of the enemy riflemen sniping the wounded who showed any sign of life, and making target practice of the dead. He will feel again the burning rays of the brilliant midday sun, and see again on every hand in dreadful No Man's Land those glittering triangles, every triangle a symbol of dead, dying, and wounded. He will think of the parched lip and throat, and hearts of anguish, pain, and suffering, and then of the welcome sunset and more welcome shades of night, which enabled the living and hysterical wounded to reach our lines, some by crawling, some by crouching runs, and some by painful dragging of bodies.

It is impossible to describe the horrors of this day. No brilliant victory can be portrayed—"'Tis true, 'tis pity; pity 'tis, 'tis true"—but deeds of valour can be inscribed, and the gallantry of the handfuls of heroes who waged battle in the streets of the village can never be effaced.

Cold, matter-of-fact official messages, reproduced in sequence as below, graphically describe the anxiety and uncertainty in these everlasting moments:

Telegram received by 94th Infantry Bde. 10.25 a.m.:
" Germans shelling SERRE."

Received 10.27 a.m.:
" Following information received: 56th Division from HEBUTERNE have gone right through, and are flanking ROSSIGNOL WOOD. 165th R.F.A. Bde. report that infantry has taken SERRE. At 9.45 a.m. our men were seen carrying what looked like machine-guns in front of PENDANT COPSE; also three or four hundred of our men advancing on the line PENDANT COPSE-SERRE."

Received 10.40 a.m.:
" It appears that 12th York and Lancs., 11th East Lancs., and three companies 13th York and Lancs. have gone forward, and you have no news of them. G.O.C. wishes you to use every endeavour to get in touch with them as soon as possible, by means of runners if no other method available."

Received 10.50 a.m.:
"Another report received that several of our men have been seen in SERRE."

Received 12.18 p.m.:
" Information from Corps points to the fact that we hold PENDANT COPSE and SERRE. Push what reinforcements you have in behind 94th Bde. and in conjunction with G.O.C. 94th Bde. confirm the success at SERRE."

Sir A. Conan Doyle, in his thrilling account of the Somme battle, says that an observer told him: " I have never seen and could not have imagined such a magnificent display of gallantry, discipline, and determination." The men fell in lines, but the survivors, with backs bent, heads bowed, and rifles at the port, neither quickened nor slackened their advance, but went forward as though it was rain and not lead which lashed them. Here and elsewhere the German

El Ferdan Station and the Suez Canal.

The good ship "Nestor" proceeding down Suez Canal.

The Gallant Fight for Serre.

machine-gunners not only lined the parapet, but actually rushed forward into the open, partly to get a flank fire and partly to come in front of the British barrage. Before the blasts of bullets the lines melted away and the ever-decreasing waves only reached the parapet here and there, leaping over the spot where the German front lines had been and sinking for ever on the further side.

About a hundred gallant men of the East Lancashires, favoured, perhaps, by some curve in the ground, got past more than one line of trenches, and a few desperate individuals even burst their way as far as Serre, giving a false impression that the village was in our hands. But the losses had been so dreadful that the weight and momentum had gone out of the attack, while the density of the resistance thickened with every yard of advance. By the middle of the afternoon the survivors of the two attacking brigades were back in their own front-line trenches, having lost the greater part of their effectives.

The 15th West Yorks had lost twenty-five officers, or practically their whole complement; and the 16th and 18th were little better off. The 18th Durhams suffered less, being partly in reserve. Of the 94th Brigade, the two splendid leading battalions, the 11th East Lancashires and 12th York and Lancasters, had whole companies exterminated.

On the evening of the action the strength of the 93rd and 94th Brigades was approximately 1,836 men of all ranks.

The strength of the position is indicated by the fact that when attacked by two Regular divisions in November, with a very powerful backing of artillery, it was still able to hold its own.

And now let us read the story in detail:

3.45 a.m.—Lieut. C. Elam reported battalion in position in the assembly trenches. Delay of 2½ hours owing to bad condition of trenches. The eastern end of Nairne found to be considerably blown in. Front line badly smashed throughout its length. Monk and Campion trenches in a wretched state. Telephonic communication with brigade found to be cut. Hereafter the only means of communication was runners.

4.5 a.m.—Daylight, and the enemy commenced to shell John Copse and front line shelling very violent. In view of this, had the enemy been warned of the attack by observing gaps cut in our wire and the tapes laid out in No Man's Land? If so, this meant at least three and a half hours warning of the attack. "A" Company reported no sign of the tape which was laid during the night. It had apparently been removed.

6.0 a.m.—"C" Company report guns firing short on the front line between John and Luke Copses, causing casualties.

6.30 a.m.—"C" Company report heavy shelling. Eight men killed and six men wounded, principally No. 12 platoon.

7.20 a.m.—The first waves of "A" and "C" Companies proceeded into No Man's Land and lay down about 100 yards in front of our trenches under cover of intense bombardment. Casualties not heavy up to this point. The bombardment reached its zenith. It was terrific. The massed guns, great and small, were thundering their hardest. The noise was no longer a gigantic discord. It became a terrible rhythm, like some superhuman machinery. It drummed in the ears till the men were nearly deaf. The air was full of hurtling death, a constant stream of shells. The suspense during the last few minutes was intense.

7.29 a.m.—The second wave moved forward and took up a position about 30 yards in rear of the first wave. The enemy started an artillery barrage commencing at Monk and gradually brought it forward to the front line where it finally settled. The German front line was manned (about one man per yard) by men who had either been lying behind the parados of the fire trench or who had emerged from shelter.

The Gallant Fight for Serre. 63

7.30 a.m.—The signal came at last. It was impossible in the tremendous din to pass the message. The troops signalled to each other. The barrage lifted from the German front line, and the first and second waves moved forward to the assault. The third and fourth waves climbed over the top of the parapet. All halted up there in the face of the enemy, just for a second or two, so that they could get into line, and then they started forward at a quick step across the open towards their objective, in section columns. It was a wonderful sight, the waves of humanity going steadily and grimly across No Man's Land. They were advancing just "as if they were on parade." They had to pass through a terrible curtain of shell fire, and German machine-guns were rattling out death from two sides. But the lines, growing ever thinner, went on unwavering. Here and there a shell would burst right among the attackers, and when the smoke cleared slightly the line would be still thinner. Whole sections were destroyed; one section of 14 platoon was killed by concussion, all the men falling to the ground without a murmur. The left half of " C " Company was wiped out before getting near the German wire, and on the right few of the men who reached the wire were able to get through. As soon as our barrage had lifted from their front-line, the Germans, who had been sheltering in dug-outs, immediately came out and opened rapid fire. Only a few were seen to retire to their second and third lines. The third and fourth waves suffered so heavily that by the time they had reached No Man's Land they had lost at least half their strength. The German front-line wire was found to be very strong, particularly on the left. A few men of the "A" and " C " Companies managed to enter the German trenches on the right of the attack, but in all other parts of the line the troops were held up and shot down. The few survivors took shelter in shell-holes in front of the German wire and remained there until they could get back under cover of darkness. What torture the troops endured in the shell-holes they alone knew.

64   History of The Sheffield City Battalion.

8.35 a.m.—Fighting in progress in German front line trench. Enemy put shrapnel into his own front line.

8.45 a.m.—The enemy barrage in our front line exceptionally intense. 13th Y. and L. suffer heavy casualties when attempting to go to the aid of the 11th East Lancs. Regiment. They were not able to get beyond our front line, and were ultimately ordered to reform in Monk trench. The enemy's barrage at this particular time appeared to be remarkably well observed, and it was invariably concentrated on trenches where troops were massed.

9.5 a.m.—Six platoons of the 14th Y. and L. reported making good progress under heavy fire, with our left flank fire trench facing north. They were only seen as far as the German second line trench, until by 10.35 a.m. there were apparently none of them left to carry on.

9.18 a.m.—German artillery firing on his second line.

10.15 a.m.—The German barrage on his first and second lines removed, and German bombing parties seen to work up communications into front line.

10.30 a.m.—Major A. R. Hoette wounded in John Copse.

10.45 a.m.—At odd intervals small groups of Germans seen in their first line, standing up on the fire step shooting at the wounded and the dead.

1.0 p.m.—Battalion H.Q.'s moved to Mark Copse, as John Copse was full of wounded.

8.21 p.m.—Battalion reply to Brigade message inquiring as to strength, ammunition, bombs, Lewis guns, &c.: "Strength of battalion—10 men unwounded. These are runners and signallers. Have no Lewis guns. 3,000 rounds S.A.A. 350 bombs. Lewis gun pans nil."

10.0 p.m.—It appeared certain that small parties of the Battalion penetrated to the third and fourth German lines, and that a few ultimately reached Serre. Furthermore, three officers reported that at half-past ten in the morning the enemy turned his own artillery on Serre, 700 yards behind his own front line.

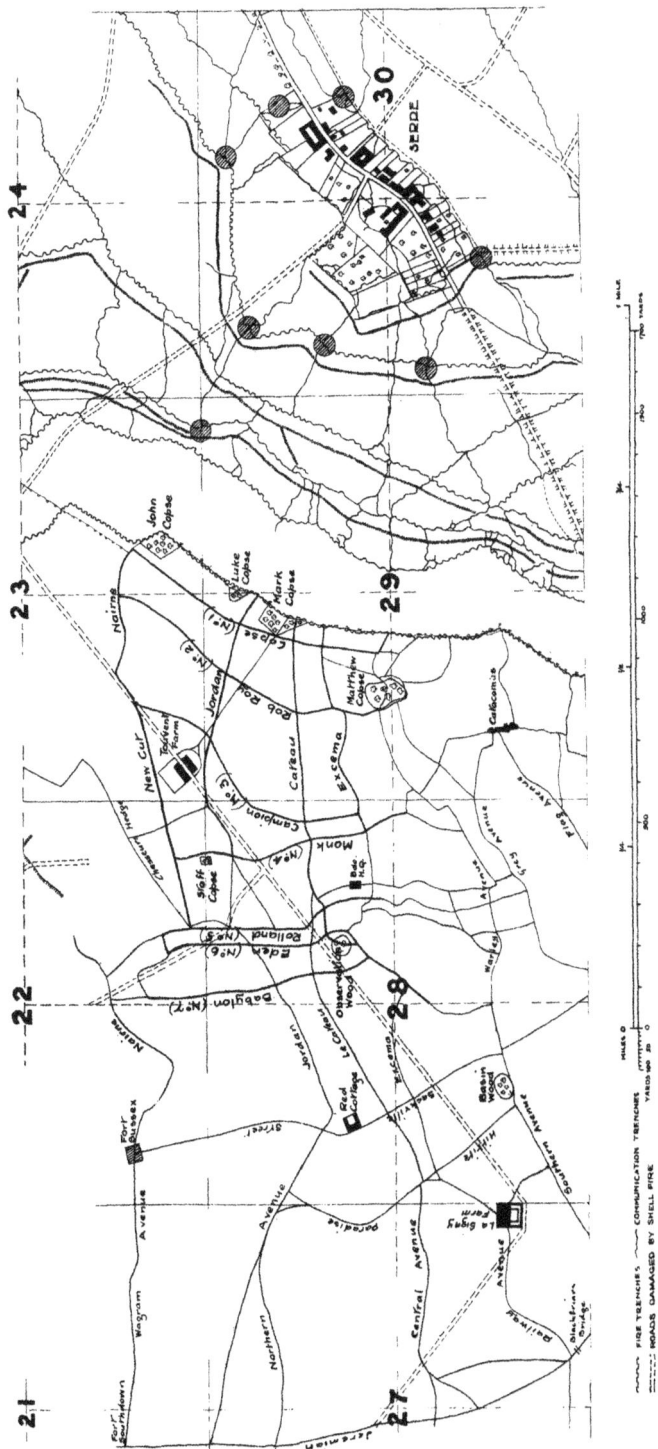

SKETCH OF THE TRENCHES WHERE THE CITY BATTALION MEN FELL ON JULY 1st, 1916.

The Gallant Fight for Serre. 65

1.30 a.m. to 3.15 a.m., July 2nd.—Messages received saying information had come to hand that about 150 of our men had penetrated the front line opposite Mark Copse, and were still maintaining their position in the German front line. Every effort was to be made to get into touch with them and withdraw them. Two officer patrols were sent out from Mark Copse with men borrowed from 14th Y. and L. These went out into No Man's Land and approached the German wire. No signs of any fighting were apparent, and wounded men who were met and brought in stated that any men left in the trenches had become casualties and unable to offer further resistance. Patrols consequently withdrew. German machine-guns were very active sweeping No Man's Land, and a large number of Verey lights was sent up. Lieut. H. Oxley was slightly wounded.

In the Sheffield Year Book and Record of 1917 Sgt. Howard Sleigh wrote:

The spirit of that unhurried advance! Take it from poor Crozier, Sgt. Crozier, of " C " Company, whose singing had cheered many a dull hour in camp and bivouac. " Why, the beggars can't shoot for nuts," he cried, with his gay, infectious laugh, as the bullets went humming past. " Look how they're missing us! Come on! And, head up, he went on, until there came the bullet which he did not hear.

Captain Clark was killed at the head of "A" Company. Lieut. Elam was not seen again. Lieut. Earl was wounded. 2nd Lieut. Perkin, small but full of pluck, was right up to the German wire when he was struck down.

Some of the best blood in the regiment was shed like water. I think of E. S. Curwen, late classical master at Rotherham Grammar School, M.A. of Oxford—just on the point of receiving a long-delayed commission. Wounded, he sat on the smoking edge of a shell-crater shouting " Come on! " till at last he was hit again and killed.

Warm-hearted little "Atty" Atkinson, just made company sergeant-major, was among the casualties, along with some of the best athletes we had. But some got forward. Big " Bob " Seymour—Arabic interpreter on a shilling a day

66   History of The Sheffield City Battalion.

in Egypt—found himself held up by a tough maze of uncut German wire. Not troubling about cover, he knelt down, as he might have done for aiming practice in the old lines at Ripon, and fired at the shouting Boche on the other side of the wire. The Boches were leaning over their parapet, hurling bombs or emptying their rifles into No Man's Land as fast as they could. None of the Germans wore any equipment, so that they had great freedom of movement. Seymour pumped lead into them until an enemy shot smashed his jaw.

Near him stood Sgt. Gallimore. Held back by the same wire, he stood erect, firing at the Germans like a man possessed and forgetful of all risks. How he escaped with his life is a mystery. Eventually he collected a few men into a shell-hole, and as long as this party could see Germans they let them have all they could give. It was under cover of night Sgt. Gallimore brought his party back. More than one of them had been wounded.

None of these men knew what was happening more than a very short distance away. Every time they raised their heads to fire they risked death from bomb or bullet. Thus it was with all who went over and came back—a sadly small band. They leave the final fate of the others who went beyond an unsolved problem.

I have written of "A" Company. Not an atom behind in the "Stick it" spirit were the others. Captain Moore, of "B" Company, was soon hit and out of action.

Company Sergeant-Major Loxley, who had gone through the South African war with the King's Royal Rifles, was lost; so was Lieut. A. J. Beal, with many others; but, ever a hard-bitten lot, "B" Company did credit to their old commander, Major Plackett, and to the Chesterfield and Penistone districts, from which many of them came.

Pte. Wenman had an extraordinary experience. He had been servant to Major Clough during most of the period of training. An officer's servant in these days of scientific fighting is hardly expected to make a brilliantly successful warrior when an off-chance brings him into the line. But Wenman got right over the stoutly-defended German line,

The Gallant Fight for Serre.

bayoneted three of the enemy, and, later on, finding himself alone, returned to our trenches, and with a whole skin at that.

The commander of " C " Company, the veteran, well-remembered Captain W. A. Colley, appeared to be struck by a shell. His men say he had expressed a premonition of his death; but he was one of the quickest out of the trench, and went to his fate like a brave English gentleman.

Lieut. H. W. Pearson, who had for a long time been a most popular acting-adjutant, and who is known to most golfers and motorists in Sheffield, was badly hit, but breezily encouraged his men.

A heavy loss was sturdy Arthur Bilbey, the company sergeant-major. A veteran of the Matabele War, he was a merry soul and a true soldier—one of that precious little leaven of old Regulars, headed by R.S.M. Charles Polden, who did so much to make the Battalion what it was.

" D " Company lost, wounded, Major Hoette, Lieut. Ingold, and that fine swimmer and Rugby footballer, Lieut. Storry; while a prince of good fellows and the best athlete in the regiment was killed in 2nd Lieut. E. M. Carr.

A corporal of " D " Company, who reached the Boche wire and remained all day in a well-peppered shell-hole, told me that he did not think more than one in twenty of his company slipped through the ferocious German shell barrage near our wire. One of those to go under was Walter Thompson, an old West Riding Artilleryman, who understudied the " great " Kirk for provost duty and afterwards became the regimental police sergeant. When he returned to duty in the ranks he proved a non-commissioned officer of the highest quality. But the deluge of war spared few.

Another " D " Company man, Will Taylor, the dandy of his hut at Redmires, was amongst those who were able to get fairly at the throat of the Boche. A bomber, he was seen to leap into the deep German trench and, hurling his " No. 5's " like a fury, drive the enemy pell-mell before him.

What was his fate? There may be some German alive who knows, but we, his old friends, who used to chaff him about the parting of his hair, know no more of him.

This is a jumbled, vague story which has been told. But no clear narrative seems to be possible. The record consists merely of fragments picked up and pieced together: from what the men tell me of their little bits of the battle, from what one saw through the waving July grass on a trench top, from what the observers and the airmen saw in brief glimpses through the murky cloud of dust and smoke. In the regimental records there is a long list of well-remembered men with nothing but the word " missing " marked against them. They went, and they did not come back. That is all.

It is so different from one's dreams. Many a day in the training camps and on the march one had looked hopefully, imaginatively, along the lines of this splendid regiment. Picked men all, full of talent, confident and fit, one thought that when the day of action came there would be many stories to tell of great deeds accomplished. There were to be tales which the people of the city would tell to their children down generations to come. But it cannot be like that.

But thrilling deeds were done. Parties of our men were seen fighting in the German front and second line trenches. More than an hour after the assault the Boche was experiencing so much trouble from them that he burst shrapnel over his own trenches. Eventually he sent more bombers from the rear to work up to the front line.

Meanwhile our airmen persistently reported that bodies of our men had pushed right through the German defences and had entered what our artillery had left of Serre village.

Not many got so far. But methinks, to use a homely phrase, those boys played steam. I doubt if any Englishman can tell you what they did, but I can tell you what the Boche did, and you may form your own conclusions. At half-past ten in the morning he turned his artillery on to Serre—seven hundred yards behind his own front line.

There are, of course, men of the Battalion whose names are already well known as recipients of honours for bravery.

Friends of the Battalion are proud of B. Corthorn, G. C. Wright, and S. Matthews, who gained the Distinguished Conduct Medal for gallant conduct and devotion to duty; and of M. Burnby, C. S. Garbutt, H. C. Arridge,

Crown Copyright] THE SUCRERIE, SERRE. [Photo: Imperial War Museum

The Gallant Fight for Serre. 69

S. Vickers, A. Downing, and R. Marsden, who won Military Medals. All these were what are called "immediate awards" given for deeds standing out.

There is much more that might be told. Of the devotion of the regimental stretcher-bearers, of the many wounded who refused to be attended to until others whom they thought more badly hurt had been bound up; of the volunteers who pressed into No Man's Land seeking wounded men in the nights after the battle (we owe some men of Barnsley thanks for this, too); of the risks taken to carry food and water to casualties; of the sad scenes at the burial of old comrades.

Those recommended for honours and their deeds were as appended:

Captain and Adjutant N. L. Tunbridge.—During the four days July 1st to 4th, in the Colincamps sector, he carried on the duties of adjutant under heavy bombardment, and after every officer in the Battalion except one had become a casualty early on the morning of July 1st. On the night of July 1st-2nd he volunteered to take out a party into No Man's Land in search of wounded, and was the means of bringing in several. His gallantry and devotion to duty inspired the remnants of the Battalion in the re-organization of the defences of the line.

Lieut. E. C. Cunnington, R.A.M.C.—For three days and nights this medical officer showed the greatest devotion to duty, working day and night dressing and evacuating wounded. Each night he spent several hours collecting and attending to wounded in our own wire and front line trench. He exposed himself to the greatest risks in the performance of his duty.

12/481 **Regimental Sergeant-Major C. Polden.**—This warrant officer showed particular devotion to duty, and personally conducted a party of bomb-carriers to Battalion Headquarters from the Battalion dump, having several men killed on the way.

12/338 Pte. B. Corthorn, D.C.M.—Was one of a Lewis gun team which went up with the third wave of the attack. They got their gun into action within twenty yards of the first German line. All but Pte. Corthorn were gradually picked off by enemy snipers and machine-guns. Pte. Corthorn, however, succeeded in digging himself in in a shell-crater with his entrenching tool, and continued to sweep the enemy parapet, giving particular attention to an enemy machine-gun in the front-line trench until all his ammunition was expended. He then remained in his position with Pte. Brooks, one of his team, who was mortally wounded, until he (Brooks) died. Corthorn finally retired after nightfall to our own lines with his gun intact.

12/1521 Pte. A. Greenaway.—Pte. Greenaway proceeded with the third wave of the attack, and when the attack was held up he proceeded from shell-hole to shell-hole, removing wounded men from the open and placing them in shell-holes where they were safe from snipers. He was seen to render first aid to several wounded men, this being done at great risk to his own life as the enemy snipers were very active sniping at wounded men.

12/275 Pte. G. C. Wright, D.C.M.—As Battalion runner he was given a message to take from Battalion Headquarters in John Copse to Brigade Headquarters in Dunmow, a distance of nearly half a mile. He delivered his message, although subjected to heavy shell fire, being three times blown up by the concussion of shells and considerably shaken. Immediately after delivery of his message this soldier collapsed.

12/1164 Lce.-Cpl. M. B. Burnby, 12/923 Pte. C. S. Garbutt, 12/24 Pte. H. C. Arridge, all M.M.—These men were members of a Lewis gun team, and proceeded with the first wave of the attack. Two men of their team were wounded whilst going over. They got their gun into action in a shell-hole, and continued to fire and to throw bombs against an enemy machine-gun emplacement until their ammunition was exhausted. They were heavily bombed by the enemy, but finally managed to bring their gun back intact after nightfall.

The Gallant Fight for Serre. 71

12/233 **Pte. J. W. Skidmore.**—This soldier, who was an orderly at Battalion Headquarters, rendered particularly valuable services in helping to collect from the front line and administer to the needs of wounded men in the sap in Mark Copse. For thirty-six hours, unaided, he attended the wounded and managed to keep alive twelve severely wounded men until they could receive medical attention.

12/1376 **Pte. R. Gorrill.**—Proceeded with the first wave of the attack. On arrival at the German wire it was found to be very thick and impossible to get through. He, with five other men, one of whom was seriously wounded, took cover in a shell-hole. While here they were bombed by one of the enemy, and Pte. Gorrill, exposing himself, shot him. After nightfall Pte. Gorrill urged the unwounded men to leave the shell-hole, saying that he would follow. This they did, getting back to our own lines. He himself remained alone with the wounded men for three days and nights, suffering great privations. He finally left to try and get help.

12/476 **Cpl. F. Peet.**—For devotion to duty whilst in charge of the regiment's stretcher-bearers.

12/1414 **Pte. W. Dalton.**—This soldier was the sole survivor of a party of carriers, taking up a supply of bombs to Battalion Headquarters in John Copse from Battalion dump. They were heavily shelled and under machine-gun fire whilst carrying these out. Pte. Dalton showed no trace of fear.

12/727 **Pte. S. Matthews, D.C.M.**—This man, a stretcher-bearer, remained in sap in John Copse dressing wounded men for three days and nights. Of the remainder of his squad one was killed and two wounded.

12/551 **Pte. A. Wenman.**—This private succeeded in effecting an entry into the German front-line trench, and bombed a dug-out containing eight Germans. He was able to give useful information as to construction of the German trench.

12/443 **Pte. R. Marsden, M.M.**—As a Battalion runner, Pte. Marsden was delivering a message when he was partially buried by a shell. He extricated himself and delivered the message.

72   History of The Sheffield City Battalion.

12/354 **Pte. A. Downing, M.M.**—A Battalion runner at Battalion H.Q. in John Copse, he successfully delivered two messages to Brigade Headquarters under heavy fire.

Marshal Joffre, Earl Haig, and the Army Corps Commander all expressed their appreciation of the effort in which the regiment shared. "I rejoice," said the Corps Commander, "to have had the privilege of commanding such a band of heroes as the corps have proved themselves to be."

The official casualty report was as under:—

Officers—Killed: Captain W. A. Colley, Captain W. S. Clark, 2nd Lieut. C. H. Wardill, 2nd Lieut. E. M. Carr, 2nd Lieut. P. K. Perkin, Lieut. C. Elam, 2nd Lieut. A. J. Beal, 2nd Lieut. F. Dinsdale.

Wounded: Major A. Plackett, Major A. R. Hoette, Captain R. E. J. Moore, Lieut. C. H. Woodhouse, Lieut. G. H. J. Ingold, Lieut. F. C. Earl, Lieut. F. W. S. Storry, Lieut. H. W. Pearson, Lieut. H. Oxley.

Four officers survived the ordeal: Captain and Adjutant N. L. Tunbridge, Lieut. E. L. Moxey, 2nd Lieut. C. C. Cloud, and the Medical Officer (Lieut. E. C. Cunnington). The last-named was killed on March 23rd, 1918, at Bullecourt whilst getting a convoy of wounded away before the arrival of the enemy.

		Companies.			Batt.
Other Ranks—	A.	B.	C.	D.	Ttl.
Killed	6	15	8	16	45
Missing, afterwards reported killed	44	44	71	42	201
Died of wounds	1	2	2	7	12
Wounded	76	62	43	56	237
Prisoners of war	1	—	—	1	2
	128	123	124	122	497

The foregoing do not include about 75 men who were only slightly wounded.

The Gallant Fight for Serre.

Actually, the whole Battalion casualties, including everybody, sick and wounded, were over 600. The Divisional casualties were over 12,000.

The " Missing "! Let us honour them by repeating the words of Swift:

"Men who lived and died without a name
Are the chief heroes in the sacred list of fame."

Sufficient emphasis cannot be laid on the very exceptional character of many of the great-hearted and talented men (particularly of "A" Company) who fell in this memorable fight; nor will it ever be appreciated to the full what Britain and Sheffield lost by their death. Some of these boys were learning Italian and reading Dante at Kantara!

Sergt. J. W. Streets and Corpl. Alexander Robertson, whose poems I have quoted, were men of unusual attainments and promise, and in 1914 Robertson was Lecturer in History at the Sheffield University. In a preface to Streets' volume, "The Undying Splendour," Halloway Kyle, of "The Poetry Review," gives an illuminating letter, in which Streets explained

"They were inspired while I was in the trenches, where I have been so busy that I have had little time to polish them. I have tried to picture some thoughts that pass through a man's brain when he dies. I may not see the end of the poems, but hope to live to do so. We soldiers have our views of life to express, though the boom of death is in our ears. We try to convey something of what we feel in this great conflict to those who think of us, and sometimes, alas! mourn our loss. We desire to let them know that in the midst of our keenest sadness for the joy of life we leave behind, we go to meet death grim-lipped, clear-eyed, and resolute-hearted."

In a Special Order of the Day, Brigadier-General H. C. Rees, D.S.O., prior to handing over the command of the 94th Infantry Brigade to Brigadier-General T. Carter Campbell, D.S.O., said:

"In giving up the command of 94th Brigade I wish to express to all ranks my admiration of their behaviour. I have been in many battles in this war, and nothing more magnificent has come under my notice. The waves went forward as if on a drill parade, and I saw no man turn back or falter. I bid good-bye to the remnants of as fine a brigade as has ever gone into action."

On July 4th the Battalion left the line, taking up billets at Louvencourt. Captain D. C. Allen, who had rejoined from the 4th Army School, took over the command.

On July 6th the Battalion marched to Longuevillette, near Doullens, on the 8th entrained at Frévent for Steenbecque, and on the 10th, after the most tiring march ever experienced, billeted in Merville, now a mass of ruins, then a beautiful, pleasant country town. Whilst at Merville the G.O.C., Anzac Corps, sent the following message:

"Just a line to say how sorry we are to hear of the losses which the magnificent VIIIth Corps has recently suffered in its gallant fighting in German trenches. They are indeed heroes, and their name will live for ever."

According to a statement of Cpl. Signaller Outram, of Eyam, who was taken prisoner unwounded and spent two years in the salt mines in Germany, the two last men left standing of the 12th Y. and L. (immediately in front of Serre), as far as the eye could see, were himself and another signaller, A. Brammer. They signalled to each other. Outram turned his head for a moment, and when he looked back Brammer had gone.

As far as warfare is concerned, it must have been an awful, yet glorious picture—two lads flying the flags when no help was to be afforded and all had gone except themselves. Outram says they got in front of Serre, but not into it, except himself, when he was marched through, a prisoner.

Chapter Eight.
Strange Incidents and a Winter's Tale.

Neuve Chapelle: A Raid: Death of Lieut.-Colonel Fisher:
Tanks: Back to the Somme: Nightmare of mud: A terrible
agony: The winter's tale.

FROM July 15th to September 16th, 1916, the division held the Neuve Chapelle sector. The remnants of the battalions were amalgamated for the time being, but eventually, as reinforcements arrived, each battalion resumed its own responsibilities as a complete unit. On the famous battleground of the 1915 fights our men had a quiet, happy time. The enemy was only occasionally aggressive, though his " minnies " were disastrous more than once. In the strong points in the cornfields, where, by the way, there were crosses and muskets galore denoting the graves of unknown British and German soldiers, they gradually recovered their spirit. They lived well, and we recall the zest with which we once ate stewed plums (obtained from the orchard near Pont Logy) in the pioneers' billet. The joys of Merville, Lestrem, Croix Barbée, Vieille Chapelle, La Fosse, and other little villages will never be forgotten. There are those who will never forget the belles of the village, the eggs, and the chips, and the red and white wines, above all the sparkling champagne. As Major Allen, used to say, it was "a jolly old war." Neuve Chapelle was quiet then, and one remembers looking calmly at the Mystery Wood and the famous little sewing machine in the ruin on the La Bassée Road. But one also remembers that no time was ever wasted in Richebourg St. Vaast, where the skeletons peeped out of the broken tombs, or in Lacouture. What desolation and scars these places possessed! Near by was a mound, and on it a sign, " Here lie 30

76   History of The Sheffield City Battalion.

German soldiers." From a literary point of view this area was interesting, as it was supposed to be the scene described in " The Three Musketeers " where the famous chase of Milady took place.

Whilst in this sector the late Lieut.-Col. H. B. Fisher and Major C. H. Gurney, D.S.O., joined the Battalion for duty. Col. Fisher had been brigade major of the 92nd Infantry Brigade, whilst Major Gurney was the popular officer of the 13th (Barnsley) Batt. York and Lancaster Regiment. So long as the Battalion existed no officers were more popular than these. The men were devoted to them.

Other notable officers who joined the Battalion were the intrepid Captain G. C. M. L. Pirkis and the late Captain V. S. Simpson, M.C. The bravery of these officers in later months became a feature of the Battalion's activities.

On August 1st, General Sir Charles Munro, G.C.M.G., K.C.B., G.O.C. First Army, who afterwards proceeded to take charge of the evacuation operations at Gallipoli, inspected the Battalion while training.

Rumania entered the war in August, 1916, and one smiles at the recollection of Lieut. E. L. Moxey taking out the notice board to the German wire, informing the enemy of our new Ally.

On September 10th the Battalion made a successful raid on the enemy trenches at Neuve Chapelle. Valuable information was gained, though no prisoners fell into our hands. The Germans had a dummy front-line trench, and naturally this had drawn all our preliminary artillery fire. The Battalion losses were four killed, one died of wounds, twenty wounded, four prisoners of war. At least thirty of the enemy were killed. It was in this raid that the late Captain V. S. Simpson, M.C., then a subaltern, first distinguished himself, and he was recommended for honour; also Captain D. E. Grant and 2nd Lieut. Thompson. The Army Commander forwarded his congratulations to the regiment. Several of the men performed good work, and were brought to the notice of the higher authorities.

Sgt. C. Loxley led a bombing party in the face of an unexpected and heavy retaliation by concealed Germans armed with grenades. He collected his men, organized

A scene in ECURIE, near ARRAS.

One of the first trenches the Battalion entered in 1916, Near Serre Road.

Strange incidents and a winter's tale. 77

bombing from the occupied trench, and eventually assisted in the skilful retirement of the men against superior numbers. When his supply of bombs ran out he entered a German dug-out, seized the enemy bombs, which were then thrown back at the Germans. Before the retirement he exploded the German bomb store.

Sgt. F. G. Earle was specially good in organizing small parties in No Man's Land.

Pte. A. Thompson.—This man carried Pte. Blenkarn, who was fatally wounded by a bomb, from the German wire and stayed with him in a shell-hole until he died. Heavy fire prevented him bringing his comrade to our lines.

Pte. Raynes.—Made several journeys for wounded comrades; also slew with a bomb a German officer who was directing heavy fire on our forces.

Pte. Stevenson.—On the occasion of a gas alarm he rallied his section, which was somewhat disconcerted, and performed other useful work.

About this time, from German intelligence, it was learnt that the 31st Division was "The Hellish 31st," and that the enemy knew that the "proud yet sullen and rough York and Lancasters were in the line." Tributes of appreciation, surely!

A day or so later there occurred another interesting incident. One of our patrols discovered a batch of letters half-way across No Man's Land. On the brown paper wrapping there was an address of a German reserve regiment and a note in English, which had evidently been written in the hope that an English patrol would come across the parcel. Attached to it also were two or three labels, and it was evident that the letters, which had been taken off English dead in 1915, had been sent to a German base for examination, and then returned to the regiment in the line for transmission to the British Forces. I have heard of no other similar occurrence.

The division suddenly received orders to move into the adjoining Festubert sector—the sector of the Islands Posts where the snipers made merry. Snipers were very deadly here, and the Battalion knew it pretty soon, for on taking over on September 16th one of the men was killed. The tragedy of this sector, however, occurred on practically the last day in this area, October 3rd, 1916, when, at 3.45 a.m., whilst trying to visit the Island Posts, Col. Fisher was sniped through the head. He died instantly.

It was very sad, for it was only at 2 p.m. on October 2nd that the colonel had returned from a course at an Army school in Boulogne. He was buried on October 3rd in the large military cemetery at Le Touret. The Pioneers made the cross and a Battalion artist painted the memorial. The artist was killed by a shell in the German advance in March, 1918. No wonder all soldiers are fatalists!

The late colonel belonged to the Wiltshire Regiment, and was the eldest son of the late Col. William Fisher, of Cardiff. He was thirty-eight years of age, and obtained his commission in the Wiltshire Regiment in 1899. Promotion came to him in February, 1900. In 1905 he was given his captaincy, and in February, 1915, received his majority, having the year before been gazetted to the Staff as brigade major. He was adjutant of the 2nd Wilts for three years. In the South African War he saw a good deal of service, and was present at the actions of Bethlehem, Wittebergin, and Colesberg. He was mentioned in dispatches, and received the Queen's Medal with four clasps.

It was on September 24th that Captain Grant was wounded in the forearm, in the course of a relief. In the old Redmires days he may have said, " Who's polished this stove? It's not been touched," and aroused mirth accordingly; but in France he accomplished much valuable work.

The death of Lieut.-Col. Fisher proved to be the dramatic ending of the Battalion's stay in this area, for within two or three days the 1st Battalion Royal West Kent Regiment and 1st Battalion King's Own Scottish Borderers took over the sector, and the Battalion proceeded to the Somme district, where the fighting was still heavy.

The West Kents and the Borderers had just come from the Combles battlefield, and they told many stories of the performances of the Tanks, which had taken a part in the

Strange incidents and a winter's tale. 79

recent battles. They vastly excited our troops, and incidentally showed what a great moral support a Tank was in an attack. For comfort and jolly times the old Somme areas could not compare with this, neither would the future sectors be such quiet ones as Festubert; but our men were anxious to see the Tanks in action.

The Scots were particularly enthusiastic. " Tanks are diamond-shape, and built like the turret of a battleship," said one. " They simply bristle with guns, and they have 9in. armour-plate and can stand up to all fire except a direct hit from a 9.2," declared another. " They're fine. Once in an advance we were tackled by a ' Jerry ' bombing party 300 to 400 strong. A Tank came up and wiped out the lot. Really, it was hellish, but the enemy asked for it."

" Do you know," he continued, " the Tanks have been on the boards for nine months, and tremendous precautions were taken to prevent the Germans getting a knowledge of them. The chaps who made them were guarded by sentries, and the sentries were guarded by mounted troops, and airmen flew about over the works."

The Battalion left Le Touret on October 5th, billeted the night in Vendin-Lez-Béthune, and next day marched to Robecq, which was more than usually " alive " owing to a prevailing rumour to the effect that the Kaiser had hanged himself. On October 8th the Battalion entrained at Berquette for Doullens, which was reached at 4 p.m. Then followed a long march through sludge and splashing lorries to Marieux, the final resting-place.

The air at Marieux seemed full of mystery. There were strong rumours about a big attack on the old front, and the Battalion trained with considerable vigour. There were tactical exercises day and night, and brigade practice operations. There was another contact aeroplane rehearsal, and all Battalion specialists received special attention, the respective sections being brought up to strength. Officers began to interest themselves in Tanks and studied the signal codes and methods of communication and co-operation between Tanks and infantry. The Tank's red disc meant " Danger or Wire Uncut," the Green disc, " Come on or Wire Cut "; Red and Green discs, " Wait a bit "; Red, Red, Red, meant " Broken Down," and so on.

The men enjoyed the fruit and chickens of Marieux immensely, as well as the wines. Little need, indeed, to mention the episode of the two men who were found in the Frenchman's cellar having a royal feast.

On October 12th Lieut.-Col. C. P. Riall, East Yorkshire Regiment, temporarily attached to the 13th (S.) Batt. York and Lancaster Regiment as second-in-command, assumed command of the Battalion in place of Major C. H. Gurney, D.S.O., who proceeded to the Senior Officers' School, Aldershot, for a course of instruction. The departure of Major Gurney was much regretted both by officers and men, for in the short time he had been with the unit he had proved an able and considerate leader, and had made himself very popular. Lieut.-Col. Riall was a Regular officer who had served eighteen years in the East Yorkshire Regiment and had come out to France as adjutant to a Pioneer battalion of the New Army in 1915.

On October 15th the Battalion received a second draft of " Derby " men—ninety-four men formerly intended for the 1/6th North Staffs Regiment and hailing from Burton-on-Trent and district. This draft, in addition to the 100 Northamptonshire men who joined on the 2nd of the month, considerably restored the strength of the Battalion, which had been run practically on a minimum strength since July 1st. A further draft of forty-eight men from South Lancashire arrived on October 17th, just as the troops were setting off for the village of Famechon. These reinforcements, though composed of elderly men possessing comparatively little military training, displayed " the mettle of their pasture " in the trying times of winter. This can also be said of the fifty men from the South of England who reported for duty on October 23rd.

Back to the everlasting roar of the guns and Warnimont Wood the Battalion trudged on October 18th, and there were hearty curses hurled at the German prisoners, who smiled evilly and played at work on the muddy roads. So handicapping was the mud on the hillside of Warnimont that every bit of the Battalion baggage had to be man-handled to the camp at the top of the wood. For three or four hours the work was carried on by the aid of hurricane lamps.

Strange incidents and a winter's tale. 81

Two companies ("C" and "D") were detached for work with the 93rd Infantry Brigade on October 21st, and moved down to Courcelles-au-Bois, living in trench shelters and bivouacs on a field of mud until October 27th, when "A" and "C" Companies relieved them. The work was done in conjunction with the Royal Anglesey R.E.'s.

In spite of the rain and the mud, the cold, and the working parties, the troops were still expected to have a zeal for training. But, then, it is a truth that it was only by reason of generals, colonels, and captains expecting impossibilities of men that the British Army achieved half of its successes.

Some of the new-comers to the Battalion suffered on October 28th. A working party, 100 strong, came under hot shell fire at Hebuterne, and one man was killed and seven others wounded. It was the first time any of them had been to the trenches. Fate!

Of course, all soldiers now realized the all-important rôle which chance, or hazard, or luck—call it what you will—played in war. The element of chance was so strongly marked in the war that anybody who fought at the front inevitably became a fatalist. "If the bullet or shell bears your name and number," said the old soldier, "you're for it. What's the use of worrying?"

Yet there was a case at Neuve Chapelle (Lansdowne Post)—and it is the only one I have ever heard of—where one of the 12th Battalion men received his shell and escaped. A shell bearing the number 285 fell on the parapet, squirmed into the bottom of the trench, and stopped near the feet of No. 285 Private E. Austin, who immediately jumped on to the firestep. The shell failed to explode, and everyone then declared that Austin would never be killed. But on June 19th, 1917, on Vimy Ridge, whilst ration carrying, Austin was fatally wounded, dying the following day in No. 8 C.C.S.

There was only one rule of life for the man who was in a fighting unit at the Front. That was—to be ready to die. Then one could safely leave the rest to fate.

At this time there began to be an increase in sickness, and during the last twenty days of October forty-eight

G

officers and men were evacuated, including Lieut. S. W. Maunder, the Quartermaster, Lieut. S. J. Atkinson (Transport Officer), and Captain A. N. Cousin (who was Intelligence Officer for the 94th Infantry Brigade). These officers could ill be spared as the Battalion was very much understaffed. 2nd Lieut. C. C. Cloud took over the combined duties of Quartermaster and Transport Officer.

It was with mixed feelings that the heavily-laden men moved off from Warnimont Wood and Courcelles at 4 a.m. on October 31st to take over the left section of the Hebuterne sector from the 18th Battalion Durham Light Infantry. The stores and transport moved to Couin.

The way was long and muddy. The approaches to the front line were very limited. The only road communication passed through Sailly and led to Hebuterne, and was subjected to much hostile fire from Sailly, inclusive, to the east. It was exposed to view from the enemy's position in Gommecourt Park for about 600 yards, half-way between Sailly and Hebuterne, and suffered accordingly. The road leading to Sailly from the west ran up the Authie Valley, through Authie and Coigneux, and was fairly sheltered; but its position in the bottom of the valley made it almost an impossible road to keep in a state of good repair during the winter.

The road between Courcelles and Sailly was often under enemy fire, especially about 500 yards south of Sailly. The other roads and tracks were well nigh impossible for the most part for traffic in winter. There were a lot of communication trenches leading to the front line, nearly all radiating from Hebuterne; but in the winter they became water-logged, and it was with the greatest difficulty that even a reduced number of selected trenches could be kept open in wet weather.

Although the walls of the church only stood about two yards high, Hebuterne had not been levelled to the ground exactly, and one could easily conclude that in pre-war days it had been a prosperous town. The buildings and dwelling-houses were superior to those of the villages in the rear, and the Hebuterne Square boasted an oval village green and pond surrounded by trees.

Strange incidents and a winter's tale. 83

The Colincamps Plain was crammed with guns, including many naval guns, and the whole sector was, to put it mildly, " very hot." It was not an unusual sight to see men, wagons, horses, and guns put out of action on the Plain, on the Sailly-Hebuterne Road, and in Hebuterne. When alone men said their prayers when passing the old church at Sailly before turning up the long road to Hebuterne. At this period the eyes of the twenty-eight enemy observation balloons were very disconcerting. However, owing to the elements, no attack was yet possible.

The conditions of the line at Hebuterne from October 31st to November 3rd were similar to those of periods which will be described collectively later. The Battalion had one big struggle with mud and shells. The enemy was now using gas shells on a much larger scale than previously. The patrols in No Man's Land had an awful time.

On the morning of the 2nd November Battalion Headquarters had a nasty mishap. The enemy, in the course of searching fire, dropped a shell on the mess kitchen at " Kensington House," in Hebuterne. Everything was reduced to chaos. Two old boys—Lce.-Sgt. Wood and Pte. Chamberlain—were killed, together with an orderly-room corporal of 1/5th Battalion York and Lancaster Regiment who was on a visit. Two other servants were wounded. The only thing unharmed by the crash was a plate bearing ten eggs. Not a single egg-shell was cracked.

The next day the Battalion came back to Sailly, being billeted mostly on the side of the hill towards Colincamps. The stay at Sailly was a period of alarms, for intermittently screaming shells fell into the village and usually someone was hit, particularly at the cross-roads at the bottom of the hill.

Four days of this, and then, on as evil a morning as one could imagine, the Battalion " embused " at Sailly Dell (with emphasis on the Dell) for a rest at Thievres, beyond Authie. The loads were thirty-eight men per lorry, with a few spare inches for breathing.

At Thievres the men had an easy time, though there was the " refresher " training to do.

The big attack of which so much has been spoken opened at an early hour on November 13th, the final objective of the 13th Corps (only one of several corps taking part in the operation) being Puisieux. It was thought a wonderful opportunity for giving a smashing blow to the enemy, who was showing signs of being very greatly shaken.

It is true that good progress was made on the right of the attack, Beaumont Hamel falling. But Serre held out. The East Yorkshire Regiment, of the 92nd Infantry Brigade, 31st Division, heroically held an advanced position for many hours; but the troops on their right flank could make no impression, and they had to come back, after suffering heavy losses. The result of the severe fighting, which lasted three or four days, was not up to general expectations, and it was believed that the enemy had obtained some inkling of the blow and had prepared against surprise.

Another instance of the working of fate was that of 2nd Lieut. F. L. Faker, a former A.-C.S.M. and sergeant of "C" Company. This N.C.O., who had a splendid reputation, was granted a commission in France some little time before the battle. He marched through Thievres with the troops of an assaulting division, and fell at Serre; a fate which he escaped in the battle of July 1st.

The Battalion was not called upon to take a leading part in the operations of November 13th. On November 12th it followed in the wake of attacking troops, billeted in the old camp at Warnimont Wood, and was under orders to turn out in battle order within half an hour. The 13th November was a misty day of suspense and little authentic news.

The next morning the Battalion went into the Hebuterne sector, and had a lively time, though merely holding the line.

The movements of the Battalion from November 14th to January 11th were:

IN THE LINE, HEBUTERNE.

Nov. 14 to Nov. 18.
Nov. 22 to Nov. 29.
Dec. 5 to Dec. 9.
Dec. 17 to Dec. 21.
Dec. 21 to Dec. 24—"B" and "D" Coys.

Lieut.-Col. J. A. Crosthwaite.   The late Lieut.-Col. H. B. Fisher.

Lieut.-Col. C. P. B. Riall.   Lieut.-Col. F. J. Courteney Hood, D.S.O.

Strange incidents and a winter's tale.

Jan. 1 to Jan. 6.
Jan. 7 to Jan. 11—"A" and "C" Coys
    IN RESERVE.
Nov. 19 to Nov. 24—Sailly Dell.
Nov. 30 to Dec. 4—Sailly Dell.
Dec. 10 to Dec. 16—Rossignol Farm, Coigneux.
Dec. 22 to Dec. 24—Sailly-au-Bois ("A" and "C").
Dec. 25 to Dec. 31—Sailly Dell.
Jan. 6 to Jan. 11—Sailly-au-Bois (Headqrs.,
          " B " and " D ").

 Somewhere in " Les Misérables " is a passage telling of a man who is swallowed in the quicksands. Sometimes in Hebuterne soldiers have realized to the full the sensations of Hugo's poor victim. With him they have gazed for the last time at the distant land with the sun shining on the hills and the seagulls swerving white overhead. With him they have struggled against the solid flood that creeps past the chin, mouth, and nose. . . The nightmare of the mud is as terrible as the quicksand.

 As one of our soldiers said: Can you conceive it, you people who have never seen worse mud than one finds around the gates of fields in winter? Can you imagine what happened when the men struggled through the slough, their haversacks rubbing damply against their sides, their dripping rifles grasped firmly in their muddied hands?

 When the rain streamed down and the clouds hung low, the deeds done were miraculous. In No Man's Land the shell-holes were filled with water, the mud stretch hid the empty tins, the old sandbags, the strands of barbed wire that tripped the infantrymen, and the mud itself clogged their steps, so that they walked slowly and painfully, dragging their feet like old men. In the trenches—wet ditches that could not be properly drained—men crouched down in the rain among boxes of bombs and ammunition. They whispered or ate, or fell into uneasy doze, waking suddenly with startled expression—waiting for the time when they would be relieved.

 Along the roads the great weapons of war passed each other in the streaming nights. The flare from a match lit up the sweating horses and wet-faced men and was reflected dully by the grey guns. In one place a huge tractor had slipped off the side of the " pavé " into the mass of mud, and the traffic was blocked for a mile each way. One by one, lorries crawled round it, while men tried to heave the great engine on to the road again, finally pushing it down altogether into the mud, where it wallowed without delay to the current of traffic.

Through the awful days the men worked on the trenches, the parties brought their boxes of ammunition up sticky communication trenches, the guns poured forth their death on the battered dug-outs and shell-pitted roads.

That is a picture of the Hebuterne sector as it was then.

There were times at Hebuterne when men fell into sumps and were almost drowned. They had to be rescued by ropes slung underneath their arms. One sergeant was only saved after one and a half hour's exertions. In their misery elderly men, on more than one occasion, flung themselves down and refused to move, crying " Let me die. I'm done in. For God's sake leave me alone." The late Captain V. S. Simpson, M.C., had two or three experiences of this nature, and used to tell the story how on one occasion he ordered the men of his company to take off their boots, socks, trousers, and pants, and wade through the flooded trenches.

Regularly men had to pull their legs along with the aid of their hands, and left boots and gumboots in the mire and clay.

Yet there was humour of a sort at times, as the following incident shows. Two men came across a dead German, and both wanted to search him for souvenirs. They let the toss of a coin decide who should search the top half and who the bottom half of the body. The one who won selected the top half and netted 400 marks.

The conditions of the billets when the Battalion was in reserve were far from satisfactory. Everything was cheerless and tainted with mud. Sailly-au-Bois was composed of skeleton dwellings, and Sailly Dell consisted of tents and trench shelters, jerry-built cabins, and dug-outs. Coal and firewood, for the men, were as scarce as candles.

Strange incidents and a winter's tale. 87

No wonder, then, that the Battalion lost a lot of men through sickness and that excruciating malady "trench feet"—feet that became as dead, swollen to thrice their normal size and in which the placing of a finger left a ghastly hole. The ill-effects of this sector were felt for some considerable time. The actual number of officers and men in the Battalion evacuated to hospital during the winter months were:

October	48
November	125
December	114
January 1 to February 7	200
February 8 to February 28	90
March	181
April	129
Total	887

Of course, over 50 per cent. of the sick rejoined at various times, and drafts amounting to 764 other ranks, together with the undermentioned officers, were received:

2nd Lieut. D. R. Hinckley.
2nd Lieut. A. R. Steven.
2nd Lieut. S. Crawford.
2nd Lieut. F. G. Morris.
2nd Lieut. L. R. Bethel.
2nd Lieut. A. W. Laidlaw.
2nd Lieut. A. L. Taylor.
2nd Lieut. J. Buckland.
2nd Lieut. E. N. Taylor.
2nd Lieut. H. Booth.
2nd Lieut. H. G. Mann.
2nd Lieut. W. Meakin.
2nd Lieut. M. B. Wallace.
2nd Lieut. N. H. Malkin
Lieut. E. G. Halpin (T.O.).
2nd Lieut. A. E. Cole.
2nd Lieut. J. M. Sinclair.
2nd Lieut. G. H. Jarvis.
2nd Lieut. F. Tonge.
2nd Lieut. G. H. Wood.
2nd Lieut. F. H. Westby.
2nd Lieut. C. W. Pimm.

Sick officers who were evacuated were: 2nd Lieut. W. H. Rowlands, Lieut. and Q.M. S. W. Maunder, Lieut. and Transport Officer S. J. Atkinson, 2nd Lieut. F. H. Westby, Captain A. N. Cousin, Captain E. G. G. Woolhouse, 2nd Lieut. C. C. Cloud, 2nd Lieut. J. C. Cowen, 2nd Lieut. A. W. Laidlaw.

Chapter Nine.
The Advance to Puisieux.

A gallant Sergeant-Major: Officer's sad fate: Nights of revelry: Towards Puisieux: A German's anguish: Land crammed with horror: Enemy ruses: An inferno: Happy Merville.

THERE were few outstanding incidents during the period under review. There were raids by other units, and rumours of raids by us. On November 27th, 1916, the Battalion's first prisoner was taken. He was an 8th Bavarian Infantryman, who gave himself up in front of our wire.

From December 3rd to January 5th Major F. J. Courteney Hood, of the 14th Service Battalion York and Lancaster Regiment, commanded the unit in the absence of Lieut.-Col. C. P. B. Riall, on leave. Christmas Day was a moving day, and the celebrations on Boxing Day were spiritless affairs for the most part, particularly so far as the men were concerned.

On January 9th Major C. H. Gurney rejoined the Battalion, but within a few days took over command of an East Yorkshire Regiment Battalion.

There were several recommendations for honours, including the late Captain V. S. Simpson, M.C., who showed an excellent example of cheeriness under depressing conditions, and always gave encouragement to his men. During a relief attempted whilst a fog prevailed, the fog suddenly lifted and the enemy opened fire. One man was wounded and left behind by some mischance. Captain Simpson immediately went back to find him and, on doing so, helped to carry him to safety.

The Advance to Puisieux.   89

R.S.M. C. Polden was recommended for his courage in the streets of Hebuterne. When shells were falling and carrying-parties were suffering casualties and apt to become disorganized, the sergeant-major personally took charge and led the parties himself. His strolls in the town were a feature of the times.

12/520 Cpl. E. F. Squires was conspicuous for gallantry and devotion to duty when a shell burst on the post of which he was in charge. All the garrison, except himself and one man, were buried or wounded. Cpl. Squires immediately took over the duties of sentry and set the one man to dig the others out, afterwards sending him back while he remained a sentry at the post.

The last night in the sector—January 11th, when the 9th Battalion Royal Welsh Fusiliers relieved the Battalion—was unique. Owing to lack of billets, "A" and " C " Companies, who came out of the line during the afternoon, rested in the almost roofless Sailly Church. Weary and grey with their trying experiences, they clustered round the many brazier fires in the church, and as darkness fell (and with it the snow) they burst into song, singing melodies of the homeland. Sentimental and comic songs were followed by church choir anthems and ancient hymns. The ruddy glow of the fires and the noise of flying shells created an impressive atmosphere.

At 2 a.m., January 12th, the Battalion " embused " near Coigneux for Beauval.

The division was out on rest in the Bernaville area from January 13th to February 7th, and a cold winterly period it was, with snow and ice on the ground for most of the time. The Battalion billeted as under:

Beauval	January 12th to January 21st.
Candas ...	January 22nd to January 29th.
Bonneville	January 20th to February 7th.

Whilst at Beauval the Battalion heard of the death of its first commanding officer, Col. H. Hughes, and an expression of sympathy was wired to those bereaved. A few days before, other sad news had arrived. A promising young officer, 2nd Lieutenant D. R. Hinckley, who had

90   History of The Sheffield City Battalion.

proceeded to the R.F.C. for a course of instruction, was reported " missing " under extraordinary circumstances.

" On 13th January (so wrote the officer commanding No. 5 Squadron, R.F.C.) a machine landed in No Man's Land, and it is believed that it was the machine from this squadron on which Lieut. Hinckley was flying. The machine left the aerodrome at 2.30 p.m. on the 13th, with orders to do contact patrol practice over the aerodrome, and although the clouds were 1,500 feet here, the pilot must have got lost in the lower clouds near by, and eventually came down through the clouds, to find himself on the German trenches to the north-east of Hebuterne.

" The enemy immediately opened very heavy fire with rifles and machine-guns, and for ten minutes the machine was played upon. The Germans then came into the open and proceeded to carry away objects from the machine. These objects were supposed to be the bodies of the two officers. Our infantry did not open fire on the enemy for fear of killing our pilot and observer, who might only have been wounded."

Nothing more has been heard of the officer.

In spite of the very irksome and distasteful calls of discipline and training, the Battalion had a good time in this area. The men usually trained until about 3 p.m. (the hour 2 p.m. to 3 p.m. being devoted to sport), the remainder of the day being free. The local estaminets, with their flowing wines, &c., did a roaring trade. There were joyous nights of revelry, when the soldiers cried:

" Ah, my Beloved, fill the cup that clears
To-day of past regrets and future Fears—
To-morrow? Why, To-morrow I may be
Myself with Yesterday's Sev'n Thousand Years."

The system of training upon which the 1917 offensives were to be based was practically on the same principles as heretofore, except that far greater attention was paid to the organization of platoons. The theory of this organization was that each platoon should consist of a combination of all the weapons with which the infantry were armed. The platoon was recognized as the smallest complete unit in the field, and it was desired that each platoon should possess a section of bombers, a section of Lewis gunners, a section of riflemen, and a section of rifle grenadiers, each section to comprise one N.C.O. and eight men. Owing to the continual fluctuations in strengths of battalions this was never possible for long periods.

Troops were taught to realize the possibilities of their weapons. They began to feel that the rifle and bayonet really were the most efficient offensive weapons of the soldier for assault, for repelling attack, or for obtaining superiority of fire. They began to learn that the bomb was the second weapon of every man, and that the "howitzer" of the infantry was the rifle bomb.

They understood that the Lewis gun was the weapon of opportunity; that its chief uses were to kill the enemy above ground and to obtain superiority of fire; that its mobility and the small target it and its team presented rendered it peculiarly suitable for working round an enemy's flank or for guarding their own flank.

The problems of battle were studied minutely by all officers, and the lessons of the Somme offensive and facts given in captured German documents taken to heart.

During the winter the transportation section of the British Army was thoroughly overhauled, and, owing to this and forthcoming offensive operations, the Battalion left Bonneville for rail work in conjunction with a Canadian railway company. On February 8th the Battalion marched to Terramesnil, completing the journey to Courcelles-au-Bois the following day. Courcelles was a very different place from what it had been when the Battalion last saw it. The major portion of the village was in ruins, and the civilians had long ago departed to safer regions. It was miserable, dirty, and sludgy, and every day the enemy dropped a few shells into it. If he put gas over, the old church bell tolled out a warning.

The advance of the railways, under these splendid Canadian workers, had transformed the whole area, and the countryside was threaded with lines and dotted here and there with huge dumps. Even Colincamps had become a prospective railhead.

The Battalion, which did little else but railway work, received further additions to strength. The undermentioned officers reported for duty, in addition to a draft of sixty other ranks: 2nd Lieuts. J. Buckland, E. N. Taylor, H. Booth, F. Tonge, M.M., G. H. Wood, and N. H. Malkin.

Incidentally, one might add that Captain V. S. Simpson, M.C., took over the duties of adjutant to the Battalion, in the middle of the month, owing to Captain T. L. Ward proceeding to a staff course at General Headquarters, and afterwards at 94th Infantry Brigade Headquarters.

The air was full of rumours concerning a general retirement of the enemy on this front, and accordingly there was considerable excitement. Whether or not the rumours affected our artillery one cannot say, but it became more and more aggressive. A man of the 31st German Infantry Regiment, in a letter which he had intended to send home, said:

> In the beginning, in 1914, I had courage, but now I have none. If you were here with me for half an hour I would ask you if you had any courage. You have no conception what it is like when these terrible shells are shrieking, and tear away a man's feet here, his hands there. So it goes on, and you must stand by with the expectation of being hit yourself. On the right and left your best friends fall and cry for help, but you can render no help. At the present time our rations are bad and we have very little to eat, no meat and no fatty substances, and nothing to smoke. You cannot buy anything. Under these circumstances one must still keep a good heart. We live here worse than pigs. For seven days I have not washed nor taken my boots off. Night and day you remain in your uniform, and the lice devour you. Heaven knows when we shall be clean again. I must stop describing my lovely life to you, otherwise, if I were to describe all to you, I should need many pages. To-day the English are mad. They're sending us comforts in the shape of one shell after another. It is terrible. I hope I shall not be hit. I wish this awful war were over.

The enemy retaliated occasionally on Courcelles, and

Hon. Lieut. & Quartermaster R. POLDEN, M.C.
(formerly the Regimental Sergeant-Major.)

HEBUTERNE, 1916.

The Advance to Puisieux. 93

on February 15th he smashed a billet, killing two men and wounding five others.

At 10 a.m. on February 25th we heard that Serre had fallen at last. The Warwicks had gone over at 5 a.m. and the enemy had flown. At 2 p.m. the news came that Miraumont had also been evacuated by the enemy and that he was retiring some distance on a large front. Our cavalry were rumoured to be at Mailly-Maillet.

The 31st Division was immediately placed in the line and took over at Hebuterne. The troops peered into the mysteries of Gommecourt Park—"A hiding-place for the devils of hell," as one man called it. Columns of smoke from distant fires were seen and ears caught the sounds of big explosions.

The 12th Battalion left Courcelles at short notice on the morning of March 1st, and on the 2nd went to relieve the 16th Battalion West Yorkshire Regiment in the line at Hebuterne with considerable enthusiasm, despite the mud.

What a " Promised Land " they found as they followed the enemy up! The scenes were indeed terrible, and I doubt whether there has since been any stretch of land so crammed with horror as the stretch of No Man's Land from Gommecourt to below Beaumont Hamel.

Numerous skeletons lay there in long rows, with their equipment on just as they had fallen in their waves in the fights of July 1st and after. Dead " Boche " were around, and here and there remnants of bewildered cattle shot in the early days. All spelt—

" The hideous wonder of a moment—Death;
So swift that he who passes nothing saith,
But mutely falls and mute mis-shapen lies."

The gaunt, spiritless trees of Gommecourt Wood on the left had been silent witnesses of slaughter. The bodies lay in all kinds of positions—some very straight, some doubled up, some with arms folded, some with legs doubled under them, some with legs crossed. Heads were loose, and some had rolled from their trunks.

It was strange how we soldiers looked on with a callous, detached air. Probably no one blenched at such a mass of disaster and suffering. In his diary one of the men wrote thus:

I visited the old No Man's Land to-day, and afterwards was alarmed at my callousness. I found that my mind had noted the fact of rats having fed on the bodies without the slightest feeling of sentiment. I found I had noticed that the teeth in the skulls gleamed in the sunshine. I found I had noticed that some of the skulls still had patches of hair, red hair and black hair, adhering to them. So matter of fact! I had remarked how the trousers and boots looked as if packed with sawdust, and how one man's crumbling thigh-bone resembled the brown, musty edges of a century-old volume. Such is the effect of war.

There were men of many regiments there, including the York and Lancaster Regiment, Suffolk Regiment, L.R.B., Queen Victoria Rifles, City of London Rifles, London Rifles, West Yorkshire Regiment, and East Yorkshire Regiment.

In exploring Gommecourt Wood the troops had to be very careful owing to enemy ruses, some of which were typical of his nature. The following were some of the traps he set:

(a) A shovel stuck into the side of a dug-out between the timbers; when the shovel was removed it pulled a wire which exploded a mine.

(b) A French stove with stove-pipe dismantled; one wire attached to leg of stove and the other to stove-pipe near by. When the stove-pipe was picked up a mine was fired.

(c) A charge of 2,000lb. perdite in a seemingly dead-end of the gallery of a dug-out and connected to ordinary telephone wires. Face of the gallery made to look like undisturbed ground with pick marks on it.

(d) A window weight suspended by flue cord stretched across the entrance of a dug-out. On a man entering the cord was broken and the weight fell into a box of detonators connected to a charge of explosives.

(e) Cap badges, artificial flowers, bits of evergreen, pieces of shell, and other articles likely to be picked up as "souvenirs" left in dug-outs and attached to charges.

The Advance to Puisieux.   95

(f) Hand-rails on the steps of dug-outs attached by wires to a charge.

(g) One of the timbers on the side of the staircase of a dug-out was noticed to be projecting slightly inwards at the top, though it was in place at the bottom. A nail had been driven through its lower end, the point of which was placed against the cap of the cartridge, which had a charge of explosive behind it. Thus, when driven home, the nail would strike the cap and explode the charge.

(h) In dug-outs constructed with casing, mortise and tenon jointed, the position of the charge was sometimes indicated by the wedging of the timber where the sides had been cut and removed.

(i) A dozen stick grenades to be fired by means of a wire attached to a sandbag which had to be moved before the door of the dug-out could be opened.

(j) Charge in a chimney, with length of fuse attached, which ignited if a fire were lighted.

(k) Detonators in lumps of coal.

(l) Book on table, with wire down leg of table. Charge fired if book were lifted.

(m) A blown-in entrance to a dug-out was not always a safety sign. Charges were probably concealed in the unblown portions. They were generally crudely arranged contact charges.

(n) A branch placed over the entrance of a dug-out as if to conceal it; on moving the branch an explosion occurred two minutes later, the dug-out being completely destroyed.

In trenches the enemy left hand grenades which immediately exploded when kicked or trodden on. He placed new trench boards on fire steps with grenades underneath. They exploded as soon as the boards were trodden on. Barricades were interlaced with wires attached to stick grenades.

The way to Puisieux, which the Battalion reached on March 9th on taking over front-line duties in front of Bucquoy, was a nightmare of mud. It was a quagmire of clinging filth, in which soldiers frequently saw dead horses and mules gradually swallowed up. How the enemy had existed and held the line during the winter in such terrible country no one can imagine, even taking into consideration his fine system of dug-outs. All the roads had been destroyed and the light railway lines bent up like scrap iron by our shells; in fact, as far as eye could see there did not appear to be a single square yard of land untouched. The earth spoke of misery and iron. In some of the craters whole houses could have been concealed.

La Louvière Farm consisted of an artillery dug-out and two tottering walls; Box Wood a few stumps of stark poles.

The whole area must have been an inferno.

And now through it all rations and ammunition, shells and guns were being brought up nearer the Germans. All night long and all day long frail men and animals were accomplishing miracles. Each minute, in spite of water that reached to the thighs or mud to the knees, the work went on. Through the murky night came the flashes of guns, the lurid glare of explosions, the sickly whiteness of the star-shells. Ammunition limbers overturned on the lips of shell-holes and mules fell in confusion. What anxiety! Working parties of men struggled in the darkness to get the teams going again—or, shooting the mules and leaving the limbers, proceeded to more urgent tasks.

It was on the 9th March that R.S.M. Charles Polden gained his M.C. for conspicuous gallantry and personal example under heavy shell fire. He had proceeded in advance of the Battalion to Puisieux during the relief, and, while waiting for the Battalion to arrive, the spot where he was came under heavy fire. Several men of other units and some horses were killed or wounded, and there was some little confusion. Sgt.-Major Polden immediately went to help the wounded men and turned out others to assist, shouting out, " If everyone was to take cover for a few shells, the war would soon be over." It was not the first time the sergeant-major had set a fine example to the men under shell fire.

The same day there was a disconcerting incident. The enemy had sent out a patrol and routed one of our posts held by a Barnsley garrison. The enemy lay in wait and ambushed our relieving garrison. There was a stiff tussle, in which the enemy succeeded in gaining his object (i.e., identifications). We had four men "missing, believed killed," and five men wounded.

The Advance to Puisieux.

Puisieux was formerly a large village of some thirteen hundred inhabitants, and formed part of the Germans' main second line of defence till they retired. There were many trenches and many fortified cellars. The village had not been levelled to the ground, but looked as if an earthquake had given it two or three severe shakings. It possessed an unusually large number of trees.

Battalion Headquarters were in German dug-outs in a disused quarry behind the first house on the north-east side of the road on entering the village from Hebuterne. This particular area was honeycombed with a series of extensive quarries. Numerous galleries connected one with another and penetrated for considerable distances. Both the inhabitants and the enemy made great use of them to escape the effects of our fire.

The Battalion remained in the line until the night of March 12th, the work consisting chiefly of sending out strong fighting patrols to find out the further intentions of the enemy. The exchanges with the German rearguards were very lively.

Withdrawing from Puisieux to the White City trenches near to Serre on the night of March 12th, 1917, the Battalion did not go into action again until May 1st, when the 31st Division relieved the 63rd (R.N.) Division in the battle of Arras. In the interim the division was in G.H.Q. and Army Reserve, in varying areas, and battalions were strictly trained in musketry and open-warfare tactics.

On March 13th the Battalion moved back to Bus-les-Artois, and for five days was under " stand-to " orders, in view of a probable operation against the enemy at Puisieux and Miraumont. It was not called upon, however, and on the 19th of March a six days march from the Somme area to the First Army area was commenced. The Battalion billeted in the places named below:

March 19—Beauval ...		11	miles.
,, 20—Grand Bouret		11¾	,,
,, 21—Valhoun ...		14¼	,,
,, 22—Aumerval...		6	,,
,, 24—Ecquedecques		5½	,,
,, 25—Merville ...	.	11	,,
Total .	.	59	,.

The bright change and general hospitality of the people on the line of march was thoroughly enjoyed, but there were many men who suffered untold agony with bad feet, owing to recent hardships in the Somme mudfields. At this time the Merville area was delightful. It had scarcely been touched by the blast of war, and Merville itself, so anxious to cater for the troops, was distinctly homely. Often since have the men referred to the glorious times spent in Merville. Unfortunately, in April, 1918, the town was razed to the ground whilst the Germans were advancing from the Lys. A few 12th Battalion men (then serving with the 13th Battalion York and Lancaster Regiment) tell thrilling stories of the dash through the blazing and half-ruined town in one of the last lorry convoys to escape from the enemy; houses and shells crashing amid a frantic, confused populace and an alarmed soldiery.

Reverting to 1917, Battalion Headquarters were stationed at " Les Lauriers "—a fine white château and farm on the Merville-Hazebrouck road and on the fringe of Bois Moyen. It was an interesting home, in that the residents claimed to be descendants from the family of Joan of Arc, and also maintained their own priest and private chapel. From March 25th to April 8th the Battalion stayed in· this district, the training being very keen. A draft of over 100 men arrived. It was obvious to everyone that severe fighting lay ahead and that open warfare was expected. As in January and February, the troops were specially trained in musketry and open-warfare fighting, companies, platoons, and sections being made to realize their values as self-contained units.

Chapter Ten.
Adventures on Vimy Ridge.

The battle of Arras: An obscure situation: Gavrelle and the windmill: Men who went mad: The Cadorna Raid: Deeds of bravery: Defending the Ridge.

ON March 31st there was a strong rumour that the Canadians were about to capture Vimy Ridge and Lens, and this, together with the vigorous preparations for offensive action already taking place, created the impression that the 31st Division was bound for the Arras front. But this fact was never confirmed before the actual event, owing to the excellent precautions taken to prevent espionage. A move was made to Oblinghem, a village near Béthune, on April 8th. The same day Lieut. E. L. Moxey and three subalterns, together with fifty other ranks, were dispatched to the 13th Corps Reinforcement Camp at Robecq, to assist in the training of the drafts from England.

On April 9th the First Army attacked the enemy's positions on the Vimy Ridge, in conjunction with the attack delivered by the army on the right. The operations were completely successful and all objectives were taken. The Battalion heard the rumble of the terrific bombardment at Oblinghem, and thereafter there was never a day that was not accompanied by the steady thunder of the distant battle.

Under orders to move at short notice, the Battalion next marched to La Bourse, a straggling village near Nœux-les-Mines, and reconnoitred the Bully Grenay sector. There was general excitement over the reports of the battle, record being taken of the big captures of prisoners, long-range guns, howitzers, field guns, machine-guns, trench mortars,

100   History of The Sheffield City Battalion.

ammunition of all kinds, railway material, dumps of stores and timber, &c.

A further move nearer to the line was made on April 14th, when the Battalion marched to Hermin. The weather continued to be splendid, and enabled much field training to be carried out.

The noise of the battle now became more pronounced, and at times one could almost feel the vibration of the intense hurricane bombardments. The skies at night were always alive with gunflashes. Possibly the fiercest fight of the whole war, so far, was taking place on a ten-mile front between Gavrelle and Croisilles, astride the Arras-Cambrai road. The Germans brought up huge reserves, amounting to 100,000 men, to win back their lost positions; but, though they obtained temporary possession again, the final victory rested with the British Army. The enemy suffered tremendous losses.

On the edge of this fatal whirlpool the Battalion stayed until April 29th, when a long march to Ecoivres, near Mont St. Eloi, was made under a blazing sun. The following day the destination was Marœuil, and on May 1st, a hot day, the Battalion moved off to trenches in " G 6 Central "—Vimy Ridge and beyond Roclincourt. The Battalion, well up to strength, came under the orders of the G.O.C. 93rd Infantry Brigade.

The battle of Arras provided one of the greatest battle pictures in modern history, and in the mass of hundreds of thousands of men, obedient to the High Command, which used them as parts of the great war machine, was the individual, with his own separate experience and initiative, with his sense of humour and his suffering, with his courage and his fear.

The scene of battle had changed during the last few days of April, because spring had come and warm sunshine. It made a tremendous difference to the look of things and to the sense of things. Before, the men were marching through rain and sleet, through a wild quagmire of old battlefields which stretched away behind our new front lines through miles of shell-craters and dead woods and destroyed villages. They fought hot and fought cold, and their craving was for

Crown Copyright] [*Photo: Sport and General Press Agency Ltd.*
A view of LENS, the great mining centre in the North of France, reduced to a heap of rubble. Not a single wall remained standing. For many months the Battalion fought alongside the Canadians for the possession of this town.

hot drink. Now, after a few days of warmth, our troops on the march were powdered white with dust, and they fought hot and fought thirsty, and the wounded cried for water to cool their burning throats.

More frightful now even than in the days of winter was the way up to the front. In all the great stretch of desolation left behind, the shell-craters which were full of water, red water and green water, were now dried up, and were hard, deep pits, scooped out of powdered earth, from which all vitality had gone, so that spring brought no life to it.

One thought, perhaps, some of these shell-slashed woods would put out new shoots when spring came, and watched them curiously for any sign of rebirth; but there was no sign, and their poor, mutilated limbs, their broken and tattered trunks, stood naked and stark under the blue sky.

Everything was dead, with a white, ghastly look in the brilliant sunshine, except where here and there in the litter of timber and brickwork which marked the site of a French village, a little bush was in bud, or flowers blossomed in a scrapheap which once had been a garden.

All this was the background of the battle of Arras, and through this vast stretch of barren country our battalions moved slowly forward to take their part in the battle when their turn came. They rested a night or two among the ruins, where other men, who worked always behind the lines, had made their billets on the lee side of broken walls or in holes dug deep by the enemy and reported safe for use.

Dead horses lay on the roadsides or in great shell craters. Dead Germans, or bits of dead Germans, were in old trenches, and bones of Frenchmen, who had fought here with the old army, were around.

Farther forward the earth was green. The bombardment had not yet torn it and pitted it, and the shell-craters were spaced and their sloping sides were fresh.

So it was that the Battalion got closer to the fighting.

Our guns were firing steadily, so that the sky was filled with invisible flights of shells, and always there came down the humming song of aeroplanes, their wings dazzling and diaphanous as they were caught by the sun's rays.

That was the picture.

At a heavy cost the 63rd (R.N.) Division had pushed the enemy back to the villages of Oppy and Gavrelle, some kilometres east of Vimy Ridge, and the 31st Division had to exploit this success if possible; if not, to consolidate the position. The Divisional Staff had only seventy-two hours in which to take over the line and plan and carry out a big attack. This took place in the early hours of 3rd May. The onerous task was confided to the 92nd and 93rd Infantry Brigades, with the 94th Infantry Brigade in support. The preliminary bombardment was terrific, and it seemed as if we were blasting our way through, but 'twas not so. For, though the extremely heavy bombardment by H.E. shells and T.M.'s destroyed the old enemy trenches, it made fresh defences for him in the shape of crater holes as fast as it destroyed the old ones. It literally blasted the whole countryside, destroyed the surface of the soil, and so enormously increased the difficulties of rapidly following up the initial success.

The enemy reinforcements were continually arriving, and, despite heroic deeds, the enemy line was not broken. The brigades lost many men, and so did the enemy. The ground was strewn thick with corpses.

During this endeavour the 12th Battalion had been in reserve to the 93rd Brigade, who were in the line at Gavrelle. It had been ordered to hold itself in readiness to move anywhere at a moment's notice. At 6.10 a.m. on May 3rd, in view of a possible counter-attack by the enemy from the direction of Oppy, "A" and "C" Companies, under Captain V. S. Simpson and Captain R. W. Leamon respectively, proceeded to Hill 80, well in front of Bailleul, and were followed an hour later by the remainder of the Battalion.

Information regarding the operations in front was very obscure, and at one time or another the commanding officer (Lieut.-Col. Riall) received orders to reinforce all the four battalions in the brigade. The situation seemed particularly alarming when the Battalion was ordered to go to the aid of the 16th West Yorkshire Regiment, which reported that the enemy was turning the left flank of the brigade. This order was cancelled a little later, however, and eventually the Battalion took up a position in reserve just behind the line

Adventures on Vimy Ridge.   103

Oppy-Gavrelle, the men taking cover in adjacent trenches and shell-holes. Headquarters were established in German gunpits at " RC 2 " in advance of Bailleul.

The advance of the Battalion in artillery formation from the railway cutting near Bois de la Maison Blanche to Hill 80 and neighbourhood of " RC 2 " was well carried out, and there were few casualties. The hostile shelling on the new positions was fairly heavy, but owing to the excellent siting of the trenches casualties were only slight.

The unit came under the command of the General Officer Commanding 94th Infantry Brigade on May 4th, and returned to its former position in the rear. Incidentally, one might mention the fire at the corps ammunition dump in St. Nicholas, Arras, on the evening of the 4th May. The flames, with which were intermixed thousands of Verey lights and rockets, leapt to a tremendous height. Bursting shells flew in all directions. The crackle of the small arms ammunition was heard for hours. Periodical explosions gave an added grandeur to the sight.

Until May 20th the Battalion existed under conditions of
 Tunnel and trench, smoke and stench;
 Hail of Hell to make a man blench;
 Pains that pierce and hands that clench;
 Horrors that scream and hiss.

The hottest times, perhaps, were from May 9th to 14th and May 18th to 20th, when the Battalion defended Gavrelle and the famous Windmill. The boys afterwards said that the enemy " sniped the front line with 5.9's." In the daytime no man dared to move more than was absolutely necessary, as the Germans were quick to spot movement and were lavish with their barrages. Practically every dug-out had a shell burst on top of it.

The Windmill spur was of great tactical value, as its retention by us seriously threatened any enemy attack from Oppy or the east and facilitated the defence of Greenland Hill to the south. It also denied the enemy observation of Gavrelle and its valley. The spur had to be held at all costs.

The village of Gavrelle was of great moral importance, and was of value. The gradual slope forward to the southern end of Vimy Ridge gave good observation, but had two great disadvantages. One was that the artillery could not be brought up into close support positions, and the other that the forward movement of troops and supplies was very difficult.

The method of defence adopted by the Battalion was one of shell-hole positions, which, as time progressed, became strongly fortified posts, and ultimately became linked up by trenches. The preparation of the shell-hole position is rather interesting. Digging was commenced on each side of the shell-hole to cut a narrow slit trench in a direction outwards and slightly rearwards. The earth taken from this slit was put into sandbags, and the sandbags used to build up the interior of the shell-hole.

The agonies of the defenders of these posts and front-line trenches will never be realized by those who were always in England. The trenches in rear of the posts were practically levelled to the ground, and were only called trenches by courtesy. Men had to dig cubby-holes in which to shelter, and then suffered in addition the frolics of the German " Red Devils," who used to steal across the sky, swoop down, and fire at the troops whilst our " Bing Boys " in their triplanes were away.

The Windmill could not be reached by day, and in the night, owing to the heavy fire, it was a matter of great difficulty to get rations and water to the garrison. It was not an unusual thing for ration-carrying parties to be almost blotted out by the shelling; in some cases only one or two men returned. Occasionally men would be " missing " for several days, and there is still one soldier whose fate will never be known. He was seen at Company Headquarters, after which he disappeared, and nothing has since been heard of him. It is presumed that he was hit direct by a shell and blown to atoms. One cannot pass this point without mentioning the fine work of the Transport Section of the Battalion. Every night they took rations and water to the line, across dangerous shell-pitted roads and country, and often the little convoy missed disaster " by a miracle," as they would say.

On May 18th Lieut. F. H. Westby and his platoon were going down a communicator to take over Windmill defences when the enemy dropped a barrage on the trench. The party immediately stopped and dropped into the bottom of the trench. After a time they got up and moved on. They came across a " slaughter-house." There was a " C " Company sergeant named Gould standing by.

" Where is your platoon, sergeant? " asked the officer.

"All dead, except three of us," was the reply.

The officer had been killed, but the fatal casualties among the men were only two, though the number of those buried and wounded was high. It would be unfair not to record the fact that the Sgt. Gould referred to personally dug out bodies with his hands and later reorganized the remnants of his platoon and took it forward to the line.

With such things happening the reader will well understand why water was always short at the Windmill. On hot days the garrison wept for water, and two or three men went mad. When they asked for water, all the officer could say was " You can have some rum." The rum had been sent for use in the cold nights, but was not often used just then.

The dead round the Windmill seemed numberless, and there were bodies in all stages of decomposition. All were either grinning black or ghastly blue. The stench was awful. Once, when digging out a trench a body of men came across something round. The men hit it, and it wobbled. They dug a bit further, and it was found to be a dead German, with arms folded. He had been killed in his " cubby hole." They covered him up with a ground-sheet and sandbagged him in.

Naturally, much fine work was done by both officers and men.

Major D. C. Allen was most conspicuous in maintaining the *moral* and spirits of the men under most adverse circumstances. He would sit with the garrison of the Windmill during bombardments and cheer them up, and would also act in a similar manner with parties going out on a dangerous enterprise.

Captain N. L. Tunbridge, the adjutant, rendered most valuable work in a very thorough manner. He was untiring in his attention to the smallest detail, and he did much to maintain the efficiency of the Battalion. He often shouldered big responsibilities with success.

Captains V. S. Simpson and **M. B. Wallace** became noted for their sound consistency and coolness in various tight corners, while

Lieut. G. C. L. M. Pirkis invariably showed total disregard of personal danger, volunteering for every dangerous job on hand.

12/631 **Lce.-Cpl. A. Dale, M.M.**, on 3rd May, when the position was so uncertain and shells were falling fast, went forward to reconnoitre the ground in front of Hill 80 to see if there were any troops between his company and the enemy, and to find out if the enemy was following up his smoke shells. His escapes from disaster were many, but he kept steadily on and obtained the required information.

12/730 **Pte. H. Newton** acted as a runner to " D " Company when the company was isolated from the rest of the battalion and defending the Windmill. During the nights Newton took several important messages through drum-fire to Battalion Headquarters. On one of these occasions he returned with tins of water, which seemed a godsend to the men. At all times he showed great fortitude and cheerfulness, and particularly when only one officer was left to control the company, owing to casualties.

12/1337 **Pte. W. Chaddock,** 12/982 **Pte. W. C. Long,** 147 **Cpl. J. Breathwick,** 12/272 **Pte. P. M. West** showed great courage in dealing with the wounded when the areas they were in were being shelled to destruction. Pte. West was killed.

13/074 **Sgt. T. H. Harper**, of " B " Company, was recommended for bringing up the company rations from Le Point du Jour at 3.30 a.m. on 10th May through a curtain of fire. His coolness and control saved many lives.

13/515 **Lce.-Cpl. H. Heatley** and 2482 **Pte. E. Kitching** on three separate occasions dug out their comrades who had been buried by shell-fire, and then attended to the wounded. They showed no fear and little care for their own safety.

Adventures on Vimy Ridge. 107

In all this there is not much individual adventure, except in narrow squeaks of death and the mental experience of each man; but it was a great adventure of men in the mass—inspired by a common purpose, fighting, suffering, and dying together, bound by a comradeship and discipline which gave them, by some strange spell, a greater courage than any man could have alone.

The casualties of the period were:—

	Officers.	Other Ranks.
Killed	3	29
Died of wounds	1	1
Wounded	4	127
Wounded (at duty)	1	11
	9	168

On May 18th Col. Riall had to be evacuated, owing to the strain, and Major D. C. Allen was in command of the Battalion until June 1st, when Lieut.-Col. F. J. Courtenay Hood, D.S.O., from the 13th York and Lancaster, took the reins in hand, Major Allen being the Battalion second-in-command.

Lieut.-Col. Hood went through the South African War as lieutenant in Paget's Horse, and later in the Imperial Yeomanry. He resigned at the end of that war and was re-commissioned captain on the commencement of the European War and appointed adjutant of the 9th Buffs. He was promoted major on February 16th, 1915, and in November, 1915, applied for transfer to a division proceeding overseas. He joined the 14th York and Lancaster on December 8th, 1915, was appointed second-in-command on April 4th, 1916, and in that capacity was immediately in support of the 12th York and Lancaster at Serre on July 1st, 1916.

Lieut.-Col. Hood first commanded the City Battalion from December 5th, 1916, to January 11th, 1917, and afterwards became commanding officer of the 13th York and Lancaster. From June 1st, 1917, he commanded the "Twelfth" till its disbandment.

108 History of The Sheffield City Battalion.

Returning to England for six months home duty on the disbandment of the "Twelfth," he commanded the 7th King's Liverpool, at Oswestry, till September 29th, 1918, when he returned to France and was appointed to the command of the 1/5th K.O.S.B. He was in the Second Army push with the K.O.S.B. from Menin to the Lys and the Scheldt, and after the Armistice went on to Germany, where his battalion had a section of the bridgehead, the unit headquarters being at Solingen.

During the final stages of the war he commanded on various occasions the 102nd and 103rd Infantry Brigades.

He was awarded the D.S.O. in the New Year's Honours of 1st January, 1918, on account of his fine work in connexion with the Cadorna attack, and during the war was mentioned in dispatches three times, the last time being in the final dispatch.

During the months of May and June the troops made acquaintance with Arras, and from such health resorts as Ecurie and Roclincourt saw our ammunition dumps go up, saw enemy airmen with tremendous audacity bring down observation balloons, saw shells burst near Thelus and reckoned how far off they were according to the travelling of the sound. They used to hear the fifteen-inchers travel down the valley, and extend sympathy to the men billeted in Arras because of the dust raised by the shells. Marœuil was also visited.

On June 28th the Division made a huge raid on the Oppy sector, and won with little loss an important trench called Cadorna. This attack was magnificently organized from D.H.Q. downwards, and was so successful that even Royalty in England forwarded congratulations. So great was the success that the enemy had retired about a mile behind our objective, and afterwards stated that they had repulsed the attack "with heavy losses to the British." They could not understand why no further advance beyond Cadorna was made. Everything was carried out so well that it might have been an exhibition "stunt" behind at an Army training camp. It is a remarkable fact that the City Battalion alone in six hours filled 7,000 sandbags and consolidated a trench that was afterwards a picture. Special

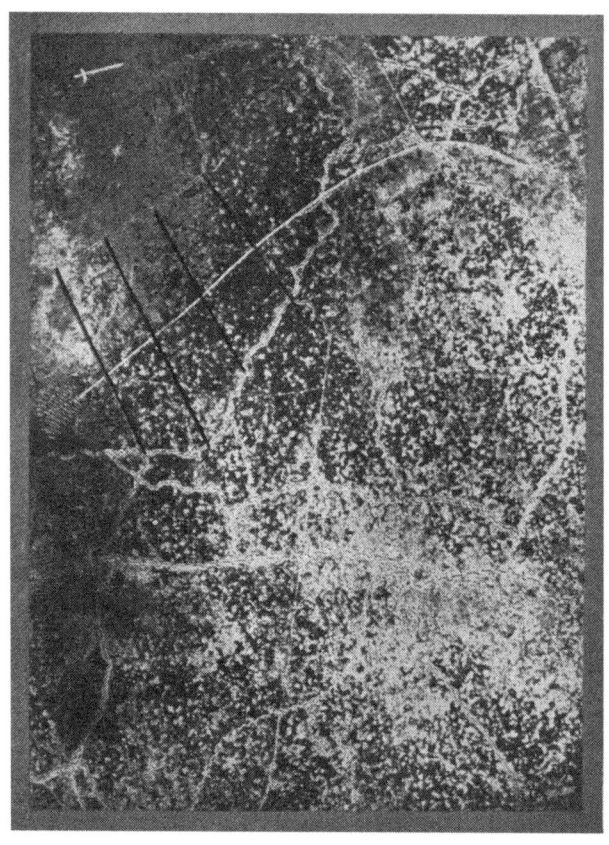

Crown Copyright] [*Photo: R.A.F.*
The scene of the Cadorna attack of 1917.
One of the actual photographs used to assist the City Battalion in its plan of operation.

Adventures on Vimy Ridge. 109

reports were rendered to G.H.Q. on the way the task had been accomplished, for the benefit of other troops. The late Captain V. S. Simpson, M.C., was the principal organizer for the City Battalion.

Nearly 300 prisoners were captured by the division, the Sheffield Battalion securing almost fifty. The German casualties were exceedingly heavy in killed and wounded— estimated to be about 500 or 600.

July 1st was avenged in some slight measure.

The City Battalion casualties when going over the top were nil, and the whole division's losses were exceedingly low.

On the 30th June the German Wireless delivered the following quaint message:

"At one point the British succeeded in forcing their way into our foremost position, but were again ejected in heavy hand-to-hand fighting. At 8.35 p.m. the British attacks began on the line Fresnoy-Gavrelle. Since the middle of April the British attacks have been delivered on the same old spot; the park of Oppy and the windmill of Gavrelle have been shot to pieces and are to-day no more than heaps of ruins level with the ground—these are memorials of German heroism. Every British attack which ever succeeded in gaining ground at this point has always been repulsed by elastic counter-attacks.

" The trenches at this point have been bombarded most intensely for twelve days. In spite of all their heavy losses, the British continually brought up fresh reserves; but the German supports received each attack, and it was only between the western edge of the park of Oppy and Gavrelle Windmill that the enemy succeeded in maintaining his possession of about a thousand yards of the ground captured in his assault."

The following recommendations for honours were submitted:—

Captain and Adjutant N. L. Tunbridge.—Did most valuable work during the preparations for the offensive and during and after the attack. He was untiring in his attention to the smallest detail, and by the very thorough manner in which he carried out his duties was largely instrumental in ensuring the smooth working of operations.

Captain V. S. Simpson, M.C., who commanded one of the assaulting companies, did very excellent work during and after the attack. He was first of his company in the enemy trench, and engaged in a hand-to-hand fight with the enemy. Later, the manner in which he organized his company for the work of protection and consolidation was praiseworthy in the highest degree.

2nd Lieut. F. H. Westby was very prominent, showing complete disregard to personal danger and setting a splendid example. He was one of the first in his company to be in the German trench, and engaged in a hand-to-hand fight with the enemy. His work later, during the night of consolidation, was alone worthy of the highest praise.

40177 **Cpl. J. McDonald.**—This N.C.O. was left in command of his platoon on the day of the attack owing to his platoon sergeant having become a casualty. He showed considerable ability whilst in command in organizing his platoon for the assault and in consolidating and constructing a strong point after the capture of the objective. He displayed the greatest energy in urging on his men in the work of consolidation and wiring of his strong point, and his example was throughout highly creditable.

14/464 **Pte. J. Briggs.**—This man was employed as company runner during operations, and made several journeys, under heavy shelling, from the captured objective to our old front line and delivered important messages and reports to the battalion relay post. When not running, he worked hard on the work of consolidation, digging and directing other men. He had been blown up the day before, when one shell caused a dozen casualties in his company. This did not, however, affect his pluck or determination.

18582 **Sgt. R. A. Jarvis, M.M.**—This N.C.O. led his section in the assault with conspicuous dash and determination. He personally engaged several of the enemy in a hand-to-hand struggle with the bayonet, with complete success, killing his man in each case. His example to the men was excellent.

Adventures on Vimy Ridge.

235226 Lce.-Cpl. B. Manterfield and **2421 Pte. J. W. Clark.**—These two, part of a Lewis gun section during the attack, established an advanced post in front of the objective and used their gun with considerable effect against the retiring enemy. On their gun being knocked out by shell fire, they went back and obtained a reserve gun to replace it, and maintained the post under heavy shell fire. Pte. Clark particularly rendered valuable services to his section commander.

12/1293 Pte. R. C. Addey.—Organized a party of signallers and completed a telephone line which had been partly run out by company signallers from our old front line but had been broken up by the enemy barrage. He established signal communication from the captured German trench to a relay post in our old front line, and did good work subsequently in maintaining it. This man had previously done consistently good work as a linesman under most adverse conditions.

12/1096 Pte. J. H. Widdowson and **6/13334 Pte. A. Bowyer.**—These men were employed as Battalion runners during the operation, and delivered reports regularly once per hour to the brigade forward signal office. To perform this duty it was necessary for them to pass through a communication trench which was more heavily shelled by the enemy than any other part of the line, and they showed the highest quality of courage and determination, never failing to deliver their messages.

12/372 Cpl. J. S. Froggatt.—For good work whilst in charge of the Battalion observers throughout the tour of duty in the trenches before and after the assault. He submitted useful and reliable reports regularly throughout the attack, in spite of the fact that the Battalion O.P. was in one of the most dangerous parts of the line and was kept continually under shell fire.

The division then went out to rest, the battalion being stationed at Bray, near to Ecoivres and Mont St. Eloi.

112 History of The Sheffield City Battalion.

Whilst here we heard of the tremendous amount of gas which the Canadians were discharging the other side of Vimy and on the Lens front; and certain members were sent to see H.M. the King on July 9th as he passed along the Arras-Souchez road. Our troops lined the route at the Madagascar cross roads.

At this point the man-power question became very acute. It was known that in future the Battalion strength would never get beyond 700 owing to lack of men, and this necessitated reorganization. Fighting companies were reduced to three and the personnel of H.Q. formed into a separate company. Platoons were reorganized also.

On July 11th the XIII. Corps relieved the Canadian Corps of the defence of Vimy Ridge, and to the end of its existence the City Battalion worked in this area. The division made a splendid reputation for its powers of consolidation, and it is worth noting that when the enemy sprang his Spring offensive in 1918 the only portion of the British line which never gave way was that east of Vimy. It proved the pivot of our line. It is impossible to give in detail the scheme of defence, but a few words are necessary. The actual front line was over five miles in front of the famous ridge, and by the end of December the whole area from the line to the ridge was honeycombed with trenches and wire. Miles upon miles of trenches were dug, strong points—some underground—were made. Communication trenches were six and seven miles in length, for in the daytime no man was able to show himself above ground. Looking from the top of the ridge towards Douai and Lens, not a soul could be seen in the daytime, yet one knew there were probably 100,000 men burrowing like rats, and that daylight camouflage patrols were out in No Man's Land. There were concealed batteries everywhere.

In the night-time all became alive. All the weapons of war spoke, and gun-flashes swept the sky and never ceased. The fighting patrols went out; the bombing 'planes of both sides sallied forth; barrages fell every few minutes; men, pack-ponies, and transport escaped as if by habit, though now and again some went up into the air. Gas attacks were regularly made, and folks in the Bee Hive near Willerval stood and listened to the whistling gas-shells going over to

Adventures on Vimy Ridge. 113

Petit Vimy and Vimy or Farbus Wood, and so on. There were the burning oil and incendiary shells.

And the working parties! They must not be overlooked. Long trails over desperate roads, with heavy loads and failing tempers, and then hours of solid work. No wonder one of the few privileges of a soldier is that of " grousing." A fellow must have some outlet.

Brigades held portion of the line, battalions being disposed as follows: Front line, six days; Red line (close support), six days; Brown line (support), Roberts Camp or Springvale Camp or Cubit Camp (reserve), six days. The camps, by the way, were pitched on the battlefields of the winter, and it was common for identification discs to be picked up; while Frenchmen were always employed digging up little mounds which disclosed equipment and bodies. I recollect that on January 24th, 1918, one mound disclosed equipment (French), a blue mug, a wrist watch which had stopped at 4.20, and disc—a " missing " man found. The subterranean galleries from Arras, which stretched right through to the ridge, were full of interest. La Targette, Neuville St. Vaast, Ecurie, Willerval, Bailleul, Arleux, Le Tilleul's cross-roads, Fresnoy, Acheville, Thelus Cave are names which call up wholesale dangerous experiences.

At this time divisional cinema huts were drawing their crowds from troops out on " rest," and one could see Charlie Chaplin on the screen while shells flew overhead. Later, brigades and divisions organized concert parties, and the one in which men of the 12th Battalion played a prominent part was that styled " The Nissen Nuts " and run as a 94th Infantry Brigade show. Quite a number of the performers belonged to the City Battalion, which also provided the artist for the scenery in Pte. G. L. Tirebuck. The reputation of the " Nuts " and its orchestra grew rapidly, and when the 94th Brigade was broken up the division claimed the lot, bag and baggage. Thereafter to the end of the war it was known as the 31st Divisional Concert Party.

The standard of the entertainment may be judged from the fact that selections nightly were given from nearly all the leading musical comedies, such as " High Jinks," " The Maid of the Mountains," " Bing Boys " &c., &c. One cannot praise too highly the excellent services which these concert parties rendered. They brought a light of happiness into the lives of the fighting men which had an inestimable influence. The occasional hour's gaiety lifted men from out that pit of misery and pain into which they had often fallen.

The Battalion suffered rather badly in a couple of gas attacks, losing over 200 men. The first was on the night of August 5-6, when the enemy sprang a surprise gas bombardment, the Battalion suffering 120 casualties, including 2nd Lieut. F. B. Wilson, who unfortunately died in hospital a day or so later. To prevent an alarm he gave his life.

The second bombardment of our line was on the night of September 30th, and on this occasion casualties numbered one officer and 108 other ranks. This attack was particularly annoying, as most of a special party trained to carry out a raid soon afterwards were put out of action. The raid had to be entirely reorganized, and when it was attempted on the night of October 5-6 a Bangalore torpedo failed to explode and the enemy wire could not be broken down. It was most discouraging in view of the tremendous amount of labour which had been put into the scheme to make it a great success.

In December, by the way, the Battalion was under orders to proceed to Cambrai, but at the last minute the order was cancelled. Captain A. N. Cousin was killed by a German sniper when visiting the front-line posts on December 6th, and his loss was keenly felt.

There was a strange similarity in the deaths of Captain Cousin and Lieut.-Col. H. B. Fisher. Just as Col. Fisher had returned from a course of instruction at Boulogne, to meet his doom, so did Captain Cousin. Towards the end of November, Captain Cousin rejoined the Battalion and immediately took over the duties of adjutant, owing to the departure of Captain N. L. Tunbridge, who had been promoted to the rank of staff captain.

He tackled his duties with characteristic thoroughness and would have made as excellent an adjutant as he was Brigade Intelligence Officer. He was an officer of marked ability, and had he lived would have made further progress.

Adventures on Vimy Ridge. 115

In January and February, 1918, the British Army was reorganized on account of dwindling man-power, and the City Battalion, owing to its numerical weakness, was disbanded, much to the sorrow of the men. Drafts were sent to the 7th Battalion York and Lancaster Regiment, the 13th Battalion York and Lancaster Regiment, the Grenadier Guards, and the Base. The band was transferred intact to the 2/4th Battalion York and Lancaster Regiment.

Thus the part of the City Battalion in the Great European War was ended. It is a great pity that there are no Battalion colours to be enshrined in the Sheffield Cathedral, but, if every other memory dies, the sacrifice of July 1st, 1916, alone will be a perpetual memorial.

Chapter Eleven.
Stormy Days of Black Michael.

Defending Arras and Channel Ports: Terrible scenes:
Heroic stand: The noble Guards: The tables turned:
The end.

MY story would not be complete if it did not contain a brief chapter on the progress of the "old boys," who, with their new battalions, were soon to receive a severe shock. They, like millions of others, fought (and many fell) in the battles of Black Michael and Mars, as the German offensives of March and April, 1918, were termed by the enemy, who thirsted for revenge.

The general line of the enemy's advance was in a westerly direction to the ports of Boulogne and Abbeville, in order to separate the British from the French. A German officer who died at Serre on April 6th, 1918, recorded in his diary: "If France is left to herself she will come to terms quickly; therefore, the main blows will be directed against the British." The preparations had been so well thought over and planned that failure was said to be almost an impossibility, and the officer was so impressed by the gigantic scenes behind the German lines, the drawing together of immeasurable quantities of material, colossal number of artillery pieces, and vast masses of men, all marching westward, that all he could say was "Germany on the march."

Ludendorff, speaking of this great historic period, said:

"For the progress of the infantry in the offensive battle the preparatory operation of masses of artillery was of decisive importance. Twenty or thirty batteries, or about 100 guns, to every 1,000 yards of the front of attack were to be engaged at the attack; these were figures such as no man had thought possible, still less had there ever been any idea

An aeroplane view of country before it has been devastated by shell fire

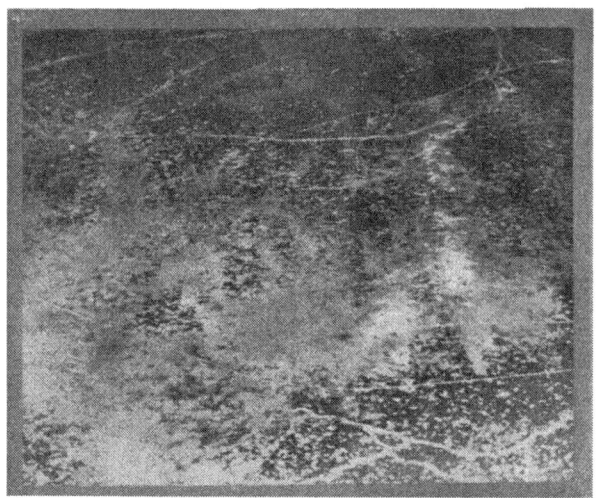

Crown Copyright)   [Photo, R.A.F.
After the guns have spoken
(Photograph taken by the R.A.F. under heavy fire)

Stormy Days of Black Michael. 117

of the quantities of ammunition that these guns discharged against the enemy. These were, indeed, massed effects! And yet what endless room there was in the amplitude of nature! Even these masses of steel could not avail to smash up every living thing; the infantry invariably found still far too much to do."

From the foregoing it will be realized what our men had to face. The draft to the 7th Battalion York and Lancaster Regiment had not been long in the Cambrai area before the blow fell, while the 300 odd officers and men, now associated with the 13th Battalion York and Lancaster Regiment, were rushed up to the line between Arras and Bullecourt, and afterwards to the Lys.

Abler pens than mine have dealt fully with these terrible thrusts. The 31st Division was mentioned in dispatches twice, once for its valour on the flank of the Third Army which protected Arras and held the enemy in check at this point; a second time on being one of the two divisions which saved Hazebrouck and closed the gate to the Channel Ports. Ludendorff says the key of the whole situation of the Michael offensive was the failure of the German Seventeenth Army at Arras. It only reached our second line, thanks to the glorious work of the British Third Army.

Sheffield City Battalion men played a noble part in these fierce struggles of life and death. Tense moments were spent by everyone present, yet, strangely enough, the silent prayer was followed by a serene calmness and occasional jocular stoicism. Fellows died with a jest on their lips, for they had prepared themselves for whatever destiny held in store.

The 13th Battalion lost over 400 men in the wonderfully steady and slight retirements in the area of Boyelles, Hamelincourt, and Moyenneville. The Guards, by whose side the Battalion fought, expressed admiration for the brave front presented by the Barnsley and Sheffield boys, who, in spite of the loss of their colonel (Lieut.-Col. G. B. Wauhope, D.S.O.), who was wounded, made successive counter-attacks.

A brief rest at Magnicourt, a village of happy memory, was ended on April 9, 1918, by a pell-mell rush to the battle of the Lys. Hundreds of lorries containing troops dashed through St. Pol, Frévent, Pernes, Lillers, and Merville to Vieux Berquin, which was reached just as the day was dawning on April 11th. What a pathetic sight met our eyes! The peasants turned adrift by this battle had lost not only their homes and belongings, but in some instances their children. All were dressed in their best clothes and carried whatever they could in their hands, the children usually carrying the big round loaves of bread in red-spotted handkerchiefs. There were a few carts stacked with bedding and odds and ends of a village; haggard women with eyes beyond the power of tears; old dames, trembling with fright, hardly able to put one foot before the other, being helped along by sons or daughters; and old wizened men being pushed along the roads in wheelbarrows. One or two ramshackle conveyances held women in travail, actual births being afterwards recorded.

Then came strings of artillery. The drivers were dead-tired. None spoke, for many slept in their saddles, and instinctively the mules pulled their loads in that tireless manner which makes the animal the subject of a horseman's love. Though mischievous and full of roguery, a mule was never the butt of a driver's scorn, for, as a rule, mules were as hard as nails and possessed wonderful stamina.

Outtersteene was reached at 6 a.m., and the villagers were making a frenzied exit, though one poor body stayed behind to auction off the groceries and sweetmeats of her shop.

But 'twould take too long to describe the retirement of the artillery and the 13th Battalion's march into action; the successful attack in the evening and the deadly German counter-attack of the morning of the 12th of April, when more Sheffield men were killed and wounded.

April 12th and 13th were tragic days, in very truth. On these days the 31st Division held a frontage of 9,500 yards and kept at bay six German divisions. Then came the Australians, but the 31st and 29th Divisions had saved the situation. As was the case with other battalions, the 13th Battalion had a gruelling time, and again suffered over 400

Stormy Days of Black Michael.   119

casualties, while men were scattered in all directions. On April 15th the 31st Division could only muster six fighting companies, though later numbers of soldiers returned to their units. One party of old 12th Battalion men became attached to the 1st Queen's, and fought so gallantly under the leadership of Lieut. E. N. Taylor and Lieut. C. V. Burgess that the Divisional Commander wrote a letter of special commendation to the Commanding Officer of the 13th Battalion. It was in this fighting that Company Sergeant-Major A. W. Bright (of " C " Company) died in a glorious attempt to win the Victoria Cross. The sergeant-major led a daring counter-attack for an important position, and was killed when the objective had almost been won. Merris, Meteren, Strazelle, and Vieux Berquin, where the late Captain V. S. Simpson, M.C., was slain at dead of night, are names stamped on the memories of all who were engaged in the battle.

Part of the personnel of the headquarters of the 94th Infantry Brigade, which was now composed of battalions of Guards, was constituted of soldiers formerly connected with the 12th Battalion York and Lancaster Regiment, and, in consequence, I feel compelled to give the details of the magnificent stand made by this brigade, which was on the flank of the Barnsley and Sheffield Battalion, near the Forêt de Nieppe.

The Guards were told to fill a gap and bar the Estaires-Hazebrouck road on the line L'Epinette-Vieux Berquin.

This they did, although out of touch with the troops on their left and right, and at times almost wholly surrounded. Grenadiers and Coldstreamers were in the front line. The Guards themselves considered that the fighting in which they were involved was as heavy as any in which they had taken part in the war. They were constantly outflanked on both sides. They were split into little detachments, which continued to keep the enemy at bay. Try as they would, the Germans failed wholly to envelop the British line—the Guards died, but they did not surrender.

One brief message which came back from a lone group of Grenadiers gives a glimpse of the scene on that eventful day when the fortunes of our troops seemed to be hanging in the balance. " We are so surrounded," wrote the officer who commanded this isolated detachment, "that my men are standing back to back and shooting on all sides." The Germans kept pressing them after this message was dispatched. At last only eighteen Grenadiers were left alive. The Germans were perhaps twenty yards away, and were steadily creeping forward. Their commander ordered a charge, and the handful of Guardsmen leaped into the mass of grey.

Fourteen returned. Still the enemy came on. When the last was seen of them they were still fighting "in a sea of Germans." One man survived, a corporal. He crawled into a ditch, lay as though dead, and crept back at night to tell the story of this last stand.

A detachment of Irish Guards came up and tried to make a defensive flank, but the Germans kept flowing round them, and, although they used their bayonets, it was literally a fight to the death. One non-commissioned officer and six men returned. A private of the Coldstreamers, the sole survivor in a machine-gun post, kept the enemy off for twenty minutes until he was killed. Some men of the King's Own Yorkshire L.I., a pioneer battalion fighting in close proximity to the Guards, are warmly praised by the latter for their resistance at a moment when every man was of vital importance. They "fought with the greatest determination, although not a fighting unit."

Another incident which thrilled us a few days later was the story of how the Allied airmen on April 26th held the crest of Mont Kemmel, in Flanders, on our left, for six or seven hours, fighting desperately in relays with bombs and machine-guns and smashing the Germans' attempt to establish themselves.

At the end of all this the 13th Battalion stayed in the area of Morbecque, Sercus, Forêt de Nieppe, Le Tir Anglais, La Motte, Hazebrouck, Caëstre, and occupied the line several times at Meteren, the pretty village which had now been reduced to a mere heap of stones and which was in front of the famous Mont des Cats, on which stood the monastery which the ex-Kaiser desired to be left untouched, but which was often shelled.

The reason of the ex-Emperor's command was a personal one. He was afraid that the aged prior of the monastery might be killed and with his death go the secret of the burial-place of Prince Maximilian of Hesse, his nephew.

An account published in a periodical in 1918 stated that at the time of the German invasion of Belgium in 1914 Prince Maximilian—then a dashing young officer of twenty— was reported missing, and, later, killed. The story as it reached the Kaiser was that he had been slain under strange circumstances by his own men.

Investigation proved that he had first been wounded and cared for by the Trappist Fathers in the Monastery des Cats. The rest was veiled in obscurity, save the facts of his death and burial, it being said that the Kaiser's nephew lay in a grave with some of his own men.

The prior, when approached by the Kaiser for a solution to the mystery, displayed a furious anger at some circumstance unknown, and flatly stated that he would withhold all information until the Germans had left Belgium and restored its shattered churches. Then, he said, he would exact reparation.

Kaiser William wrote to the Pope asking his Holiness to request the prior to return the prince's body to Germany, that it might rest in the family vault. This the spirited prior also said he would refuse until the end of the war.

Prince Maximilian was the son of the Kaiser's sister, Princess Margarete.

On large sectors of the British front the new line seemed strange to those long accustomed to the wire-bound trench zone. It had been shaped according to circumstance, for it was a line actually determined by the depth of the German thrust, which left its high-water mark of corpses and destruction. Following it came the British local counter-offensives —small, determined battles for local tactical points—and these pushed the Germans back to low-water mark.

This beach of débris and devastated country marked the new front, and the actual front-line positions of both sides ran between the two tide limits, but the ebb and flow had left their track of corpses throughout the zone.

Behind the line on both sides were deserted villages, evacuated by the civilians and not yet seriously damaged by shellfire. Support-trenches meandered about among these disconnected farms and houses, and daring men, risking the hostile sniper or the casual shell, were able to salve fruit, vegetables, and even eggs and livestock. These farms contained a pitiful medley of poor furniture, coarse clothes, and domestic trifles strewn amid the general untidiness of the homestead. Shells had brought down plaster and roofing tiles, dead Germans where the counter-attack left them, dead cows and other stock rotted in the byres, and shattered machine-gun mountings rusted among the outhouses.

Little by little, burial parties attended to this monstrous task, interring cows and dead horses and spreading wide the life-saving chloride of lime. War itself carries its own dread sanitary agent in the shape of fire, and daily the ruins blossomed into flame and smoke under shellfire, while at night the horizon was red-girdled with the reflection of a dozen burning homesteads.

No Man's Land itself held a few perfectly good, undamaged farms, veritable Tom Tiddler's grounds—too dangerous to be occupied either by us or by the enemy. At dusk both sides sent out patrols to see if the other side had seized the farm, but there was no desire for conflict, for both sides were busy digging in to improve their positions.

The line where weary men flung themselves down in odd shell-holes and behind scraps of ruins had been dug in deeper every day. First a hasty breastwork was thrown up, then in a few days an actual trench took shape, and the rough line became everywhere connected. Bouquets of barbed wire and stakes blossomed in the night, and within a month the front that had been open became again a permanent position, with a full trench system and all the defences of siege warfare.

In July, 1918, Captain J. C. Cowen won the Military Cross. He, with a fellow-officer and three men, penetrated the German line of outposts and captured two of the enemy. He took them by surprise and cowed them, even though his revolver was unloaded, and, calling on his men, brought his prisoners back to our lines through heavy machine-gun fire.

Eventually, after the Battalion had captured in distinguished manner various farms—notably Ankle Farm and Soyer Farm—it took part in the pursuit of the retiring

Stormy Days of Black Michael.   123

enemy. The division was on the flank of the Second Army when the brilliant assault in Flanders was made, and the York and Lancasters followed up the Germans through Meteren, Bailleul, almost to Armentières. Then it was switched to the left, through Neuve Eglise, over Messines Ridge, and engaged the enemy as he retreated beyond the River Lys at Warneton, near Ploegsteert Wood.

Hereafter there was a pause, but before many days the division was in rapid action again, crossing the Lys and getting in touch with the swift-footed Germans with considerable difficulty. The Battalion's path lay through Les Quesnoy, Lindselles, and various desolate lands and villages in which savage and wanton destruction had been wrought by a furious and beaten foe.

Fairer scenes were witnessed at Tourcoing and Roubaix, where our troops were hailed as sweet deliverers and greeted by a rescued people with overwhelming displays of emotion. Streets were decorated with flags and bunting, and commanding officers were presented with bouquets of flowers. The gratitude of the inhabitants was boundless, for they alone knew from what fearful agony they had been delivered.

On to the Scheldt the Battalion went, and then came back a little distance, marching to Courtrai and thereafter moving forward well nigh to Brussels.

After Armistice Day the division turned about and had a long march across famous battlefields, passing through Menin, Passchendaele, Ypres, finally billeting near St. Omer, where demobilization began.

The 7th Battalion had stirring times also, and finished up at the old spot, Mailly-Maillet.

Before concluding, mention should be made of the fact that over 500 members of the City Battalion at one time or another received His Majesty's Commission, and a very large number of them gained honours and distinctions on the field of battle.

Honours and Awards.

D.S.O.
Lieut.-Col. F. J. Courtenay Hood.

MILITARY CROSS.
R.-S.-M. C. Polden.
Captain V. S. Simpson.

D.C.M.
Pte. B. Corthorn, Pte. G. C. Wright, and Pte. S. Matthews.

MILITARY MEDAL.
Pte. R. T. Owen, Pte. R. Wilson, Pte. B. C. Wilkinson, Pte. E. Spencer, Lce.-Cpl. F. E. Watkins, Cpl. M. C. P. Headeach, Sgt. H. O. Crozier, Pte. G. Hanson, Act.-Sgt. M. B. Burnby, Pte. C. S. Garbutt, Pte. H. C. Arridge, Lce.-Cpl. A. Downing, Pte. R. Marsden, Pte. S. Vickers, Act.-Sgt. A. Dale, Lce.-Sgt. J. Breathwick, Act.-Cpl. W. Burrell, Lce.-Cpl. B. Manterfield, Pte. J. W. Clarke, Pte. J. Briggs, and Sgt. R. A. Jarvis.

M.S.M.
Sgt. H. R. Sleigh and Sgt. R. A. Sparling.

MENTIONS.
Captain D. E. Grant, Captain N. L. Tunbridge, Lieut. E. C. Cunnington (R.A.M.C.), Captain V. S. Simpson, M.C., Lieut. F. W. S. Storry, Captain R. W. Leaman, Cpl. E. F. Squires, Act.-Sgt. W. K. Bourne, and R.S.M. W. T. Ottaway.

(This list does not include decorations awarded to officers and men whilst serving with other battalions.)

Roll of Honour.

Officers, N.C.O's., and Men of the 12th Battalion York & Lancaster Regiment Fallen in Action.

Supplied by the courtesy of the Officer-in-charge, No. 2 Infantry Records, York.

Reg. No.	Rank.	Name.	Date of Death.
12/284	Pte.	Aspland, Sidney Eric	1/7/16
12/285	,,	Austin, Ellis	20/6/17
12/577	L/Cpl.	Andrew, Joseph	1/7/16
12/838	A/C.S.M.	Atkinson, Herbert Anthony	9/7/16
12/849	Pte.	Ambler, John Hayes	1/7/16
12/851	,,	Appleby, Frank Oldfield	1/7/16
12/1381	,,	Atkinson, Cyril	1/7/16
12/1893	,,	Ashton, Arthur	1/7/16
40185	L/Cpl.	Appleton, Cyril	16/2/17
12/578	Cpl.	Askew, Herbert	25/10/18
12/1527	Pte.	Aspinall, Robert	21/5/16
12/25	,,	Arrowsmith, A. E.	16/5/16
	Lieut.	Beal, A. J.	1/7/16
235607	Pte.	Brown, Harry Sidney	28/10/17
	Lieut.	Berry, R. D.	12/5/17
	2nd Lieut.	Buckland, J.	16/6/17
12/4	C.S.M.	Bilbey, Arthur Thomas	1/7/16
12/30	Pte.	Bailey, Bernard	26/6/16
12/39	A/Sgt.	Beall, Wilfred Randall	1/7/16
12/53	L/Cpl	Boyd, Joseph Martyn	1/7/16
12/64	L/Cpl.	Buxton, Herbert Archibald	23/3/17
12/288	Pte.	Bagshaw, William	1/7/16
12/289	,,	Bailey, Joseph	1/7/16
12/291	,,	Barlow, Wilfred	16/5/16
12/294		Batley, Edward	1/7/16
12/296		Baylis, Lawrence	1/7/16

History of The Sheffield City Battalion.

Reg. No.	Rank.	Name.	Date of Death.
12/307	Cpl.	Braham, George	1/7/16
12/310	Pte.	Bramham, George	13/10/18
12/314	C.S.M.	Bright, Arthur Willey	12/4/18
12/318	Pte.	Brookfield, Frederick Harold	1/7/16
12/591	,,	Bedford, Norman	1/7/16
12/593	,,	Beniston, Aubrey	1/7/16
12/597	L/Cpl.	Blenkarn, William	10/9/16
12/600	Pte.	Bowes, Frank	1/7/16
12/604	,,	Bratley, Clifford William	11/4/18
12/606	,,	Brindley, Charles W.	14/3/17
12/607	,,	Brown, Arthur	1/7/16
12/608	,,	Brown, Samuel	6/12/17
12/611	,,	Busfield, Harry Craven	18/5/17
12/862	L/Cpl.	Barnsley, Frank	1/7/16
12/865	Pte.	Barrott, John Henry	1/7/16
12/867	,,	Barton, John Arthur	1/7/16
12/870	,,	Bennett, Joseph Arnold	1/7/16
12/871	L/Cpl.	Binder, Walter Bertram	1/7/16
12/874	,,	Bland, Ernest	1/7/16
12/879	Pte.	Brammer, Archie	1/7/16
12/882	,,	Brown, Stanley	1/7/16
12/887	,,	Buttery, John Arnold	1/7/16
12/1116	,,	Black, Scott Shaw	1/7/16
12/1125	,,	Brookes, Reginald Francis	1/7/16
12/1149	,,	Burgon, John William	1/7/16
12/1162	A/Sgt.	Barber, Bennett	28/6/18
12/1163	Pte.	Bagshawe, William Wyatt	1/7/16
12/1243	,,	Bussey, Leonard	1/7/16
12/1267	,,	Burch, Percy	16/5/16
12/1383	,,	Brown, Frank	1/7/16
12/1448	,,	Beaumont, Douglas	1/7/16
12/1461	,,	Bratley, John William	1/7/16
12/1587	L/Cpl.	Baker, Reginald Thomas	1/7/16
12/1471	Pte.	Bassinder, Leonard	1/7/16
12/1668	,,	Bramham, Geo. Henry	14/11/16
12/1831	,,	Bull, Albert Edward	1/7/16
12/1881		Briggs, Reuben	1/7/16
12/2075		Bagshaw, Joseph Harold	24/1/18

Roll of Honour. 127

Reg. No.	Rank.	Name.	Date of Death.
3/2486	L/Cpl.	Bamford, Jethrew	28/7/17
16166	Pte.	Boocock, Joseph	10/5/17
22381	,,	Bramweld, Robt. Oswald	14/12/16
31354	,,	Barber, Herbert	12/5/17
31558	Pte.	Barlow, John	15/11/16
31965	,,	Beaumont, Alfred	11/5/17
40086	,,	Bell, Frank	18/7/17
235607	,	Brown, Harry Sidney	28/10/17
12/881		Brown, Ronald Bower	20/7/18
12/1180		Brown, John Arthur	9/10/17
12/1468		Benton, Arthur	24/10/18
12/1575		Barton, Harvey	9/9/17
4845	,,	Bullivant, A.	12/5/17
	Capt.	Colley, W. A.	1/7/16
	Capt.	Clark, W. S.	1/7/16
	2nd Lieut.	Carr, E. M.	1/7/16
	Capt. & Adjt.	Cousin, A. N.	7/10/17
12/68	Pte.	Cartwright, Frederick	1/7/16
12/69	,,	Casey, Alphaeus Abbott	1/7/16
12/73	,,	Clarke, Arthur	1/7/16
12/74	A/Cpl.	Clifton, Edgar	1/7/16
12/76	Pte.	Copplestone, John	1/7/16
12/82	,,	Crimes, Leonard Gordon	1/7/16
12/84	,,	Crossland, Herbert	1/7/16
12/85	L/Cpl.	Curwen, Edward Stanley	1/7/16
12/336	Sgt.	Cooper, Randall	1/7/16
12/344	Pte.	Cuthbert, Edgar	12/10/14
12/615	L/Cpl.	Chandler, Norman William Gibbs	1/7/16
12/617	Drummer	Clark, William Henry	27/10/18
12/626	A/Cpl.	Coverdale, Leonard	1/7/16
12/628	Sgt.	Crozier, Henry Cecil	1/7/16
12/888	Pte.	Carr, James Edward	3/7/16
12/889	,,	Chamberlain, Chas. Fred	2/11/16
12/891	,,	Cole, William	1/7/16
12/897	Sgt.	Cundliffe, Clement	1/7/16
12/1154	Pte.	Currier, Joseph Fredk.	1/7/16

Roll of Honour.

Reg. No.	Rank.	Name.	Date of Death.
12/1174	A/Sgt.	Corbyn, George Sidney	1/7/16
12/1190	Pte.	Cavill, Albert	30/8/16
12/1235	,,	Charles, James Randolph	17/6/17
12/1294	,,	Clixby, Cecil Charles	1/7/16
12/1316	,,	Culf, Fredk. Carrington	1/7/16
12/1388	Sgt.	Clay, Henry Charles	17/6/16
12/1702	Pte.	Croft, Alfred	10/9/16
12/1989	,,	Cave, Leslie Fred Silas	18/5/17
12/2009		Cadman, Walter Bretsford	10/9/16
12/65		Carding-Wells, J. R.	1/7/16
3/2625		Cliffe, Frank	30/6/17
21950		Coggon, Alfred Holmes	1/7/17
22258		Chapman, Thomas	4/5/17
28416	,,	Clark, Sidney	27/7/17
28426	,,	Coates, Samuel	25/8/17
37936	,,	Crabtree, Wray	10/5/17
38013	L/Cpl.	Chadwick, John Henry	18/2/18
39050	Pte.	Clay, Sidney	19/6/17
235615	,,	Catlyn, Sidney	1/10/17
235619	,,	Clarke, William Fredk.	24/9/17
12/1337	A/Cpl.	Chaddock, Wm. Myring	12/4/18
12/1456	Pte.	Chambers, Hedley	4/4/18
12/1541	,,	Constable, Harry	16/9/16
12/1469	,,	Cook, Gilbert George	16/5/16
235201	,,	Copley, B.	25/5/17
	2nd Lieut.	Dinsdale, Frank	1/7/16
	2nd Lieut.	Davies, F. A.	14/5/17
12/352	A/Sgt.	Donoghue, Frederick	1/7/16
12/355	L/Cpl.	Dungworth, Frank	23/10/17
12/638	Pte.	Dowty, Horace Bradley	16/5/16
12/641	,,	Driver, Horace	1/7/16
12/1336	,,	Devey, Rodney Frank	1/7/16
12/1345	,	Davies, Harold Elliott	1/7/16
12/1415		Dawson, Charles Wm.	1/7/16
12/1742		Davies, John Arthur	1/7/16
12/1825		Davies, Wilfred	1/7/16

Roll of Honour.

Reg. No.	Rank.	Name.	Date of Death.
31587	Pte.	Deville, Percy Robinson	3/5/17
31594	,,	Dawson, Henry	29/6/17
31974	,,	Dawson, Harold	26/11/16
38015	,,	Dunn, James Edward	7/11/16
38016	L/Cpl.	Dunn, Thomas	16/6/17
202850	Pte.	Damms, Wilfred	28/3/18
235622	,,	Dicks, Edwin James	25/9/17
12/1722	,,	Davenport, Laurence	1/7/16
	Lieut.	Elam, C.	1/7/16
12/357	Pte.	Ellis, Hubert Victor	1/7/16
12/358	,,	Emmerson, Wm. Arthur	8/4/16
12/560	C.S.M.	Ellis, John William	4/5/16
12/645	Cpl.	Eteson, Harold	1/7/16
12/1247	L/Cpl.	Emmerson, Ernest	1/7/16
12/1301	Pte.	Eyre, Leonard	1/7/16
12/1397	,,	Earnshaw, Frank	20/5/16
12/1510	,,	Ellis, Edgar William	1/7/16
12/1781	,,	Elliott, William George	1/7/16
22262	,,	Ellis, Arnold	20/5/17
21891	Cpl.	Ellis, Henry Cecil	18/5/17
12/1542	Pte.	Eadon, Joseph William	19/4/18
	Lieut.-Col.	Fisher, H. B.	3/10/16
12/100	Cpl.	Ford, William Edgar	15/11/16
12/105	Pte.	Foxon, Alan Hugh	16/9/16
12/364	,,	Fearnley, Frank	15/9/16
12/365	,,	Fennell, Ernest	1/7/16
12/372	Sgt.	Froggatt, James Stuart	12/4/18
12/649	L/Cpl.	Farrand, Hubert Percival	1/7/16
12/651	Pte.	Furniss, Edwin	16/5/16
12/915	,,	Fields, George Arthur	1/7/16
12/916	,,	Fletcher, Arthur Ernest	1/7/16
12/920	L/Cpl.	Froggatt, John	1/7/16
12/1238	Pte.	Frost, Arthur Douglas	4/5/16
12/1297	,,	Fletcher, Charles	2/7/16
12/1407	,,	Fletcher, Arthur	1/7/16
12/1453		Frith, John William	1/7/16
12/1548		Furniss, Edward Victor	1/7/16

130   History of The Sheffield City Battalion.

Reg. No.	Rank.	Name.	Date of Death.
12/1964	Pte.	Franks, Alexander Hugh	1/7/16
12/2032	,,	French, Samuel	10/9/16
12/2047		Fairclough, Joseph Seamore	24/9/16
14/1052		Fell, John William	12/5/17
31981		Fletcher, Windross	27/6/17
31982	,,	Freeman, Herbert	9/10/17
12/110	Cpl.	Gee, Frank	4/5/16
12/114	Pte.	Gill, Sidney	1/7/16
12/375	,,	Gambles, Thos. Edward	1/7/16
12/378	L/Cpl.	Gill, Wm. Chambers	1/7/16
12/380	Pte.	Gration, Frank Alfred	25/1/18
12/383	,,	Griffiths, Edwin	1/7/16
12/655	,,	Glossop, Edwin Reginald	1/7/16
12/660	L/Cpl.	Gunstone, Frank R.	1/7/16
12/661	Pte.	Gunstone, Wm. Walter	1/7/16
12/922	,,	Gapes, Ronald Ernest	1/7/16
12/924	..	Gardiner, Ernest	1/7/16
12/929		Goodlad, Alfred	7/5/17
12/934		Greensmith, Arthur Clarence	1/7/16
12/1354		Gleave, Francis	14/6/16
12/1485		Gregory, Ernest	1/7/16
12/1521		Greenaway, Arthur	1/7/16
12/1535		Grove, Arthur	1/7/16
12/1923		Gill, John Wilfred	1/7/16
22260		Garlick, Harry	18/12/16
28715		Graham, John James	24/1/18
12/1403		Grayson, William	24/12/18
13388		Gilding, John Thomas	26/6/17
235233	,,	Green, H.	30/6/17
13/1059	,,	Gilberthorpe, W.	27/6/17
11013	Sgt.	Gardiner, J.	25/11/17
	2nd Lieut.	Hinckley, D. R.	13/1/17
12/133	Pte.	Hanforth, Charles Haydn	9/2/15
12/154	,,	Horsfield, Ronald Bowden	1/7/16

Roll of Honour.

Reg. No.	Rank.	Name.	Date of Death.
12/388	Pte.	Handbury, Harry	8/4/16
12/389	,,	Harrington, Harold Wannop	11/4/18
12/392	A/Sgt.	Headeach, Maurice Charles Pilford	1/7/16
12/401	L/Cpl.	Hobson, Percy	1/7/16
12/407	Pte.	Hoodless, Harold Robert	1/7/16
12/413	,,	Humphrey, John	12/5/17
12/467	,,	Holdsworth, Jas. Edwd.	24/7/16
12/663	,,	Hale, Harry Thomas	1/7/16
12/667	Cpl.	Hampton, Fred Barmer	1/7/16
12/668	L/Cpl.	Hardwick, Stafford	4/5/16
12/671	Pte.	Hawson, George	1/7/16
12/672	,,	Haycock, Isaac	1/7/16
12/673	L/Cpl.	Haydock, John William	1/7/16
12/679	Pte.	Hinchcliffe, Willie	1/7/16
12/683	,,	Hogg, Alfred Calvert	1/7/16
12/686	,,	Hollingworth, Harold	1/7/16
12/687		Hollis, Arthur James	1/7/16
12/691	,,	Hough, Ernest	1/7/16
12/939	,,	Hackett, Robert	1/7/16
12/957	,,	Hobson, Fredk. Haydn	1/7/16
12/1141	Sgt.	Henderson, Robert	30/6/16
12/1206	Pte.	Hartley, Frank	1/7/16
12/1308	,,	Hudson, Albert	1/7/16
12/1318	,,	Hogg, Frank	7/8/16
12/1325	,	Harrison, Clarence John	1/7/16
12/1358	,,	Hanson, Geoffrey	1/7/16
12/1369	,,	Hudson, Ernest	1/7/16
12/1370	,,	Hulley, Frank	1/7/16
12/1377	L/Cpl.	Haskey, George Henry	1/7/16
12/1398	Pte.	Hobson, John Charles	19/4/17
12/1413	L/Cpl.	Hanson, Frank Cecil	27/7/16
12/1546	Pte.	Hall, Percy	28/3/17
12/2084	,,	Hewson, William	27/8/16
27794	,,	Harrison, Lewis	10/5/17
31291		Heading, Robert James	29/11/16
31295		Hooper, Arthur Wm.	7/6/17

132 History of The Sheffield City Battalion.

Reg. No.	Rank.	Name.	Date of Death.
31302	Pte.	Hibberd, Wm. Thomas	21/5/17
31618	,,	Henton Henry	12/5/17
31626	,,	Hooton, William	6/5/17
31629	,,	Hollis, Percy William	27/6/17
38057	A/Sgt.	Hacking, William	11/5/17
39042	Pte.	Handley, Wilfred	12/5/17
43898	,,	Hern, Howard	12/5/17
24439	,,	Hammond, James Albert	25/5/17
39073		Housley, Clarence	4/5/17
12/416		Ibbotson, Cecil George	21/6/16
12/967	,,	Ingram, Cecil Ismay	1/7/16
11317	,,	Ibbotson, George Henry	14/5/17
16742	,,	Ibbotson, Mannassah	9/3/17
40178	L/Cpl.	Ingham, Thomas Henry	11/5/17
12/163	Pte.	Jones, David	1/7/16
12/419	Cpl.	Jackson, Edward	18/9/18
12/700	Pte.	Johnson, Clement	16/5/16
12/702	,,	Johnstone, Fredk. Reddock	10/7/16
12/1344		Jebson, Ernest	4/7/16
12/1585		Johnson, Horace	17/5/16
12/1625		Jones, Frederick	25/3/18
12/1775	,,	Jackman, Francis	1/7/16
12/1833	,,	Jarvis, Ernest Albert	1/7/16
24497	Cpl.	Johnson, Frank	27/6/17
32002	Pte.	Johnson, James Septimus	12/5/17
235211	,,	Judge, Albert	18/5/17
12/427		Kirkham, William	3/7/16
12/709		Knighton, James	1/7/16
12/710		Knowles, Frank Kitson	1/7/16
12/1361		Kingwell, Leonard Wm.	6/7/16
12/1445		Kettell, Charles Herbert	1/7/16
12/1481		Kelk, John Henry	1/7/16
32003		Kettlewell, Mark	29/6/17
12/175		Lister, Reginald	1/7/16

Roll of Honour. 133

Reg No.	Rank.	Name.	Date of Death
12/429	Pte.	Lack, Herbert	6/7/16
12/430	,,	Lait, Maurice	1/7/16
12/431	,,	Lanfear, Arthur Sidney	1/7/16
12/435	,,	Lewis, Tom	1/7/16
12/438	,,	Lowcock, Harry	15/9/16
12/562	C.S.M.	Loxley, William Henry	1/7/16
12/569	Sgt.	Lavender, Wilfred Harris	1/7/16
12/715	Pte.	Leavesley, Sydney	1/7/16
12/716	,,	Leigh, Richard	1/7/16
12/980	L/Cpl.	Lees, Thomas	1/7/16
12/1156	Pte.	Langley, Cecil Herbert	1/7/16
12/1186	,,	Levick, Albert	1/7/16
12/1207	,,	Lovell, Albert	1/7/16
12/1780		Lamb, Sherard	1/7/16
31641		Leadbeater, Edward	16/2/17
12/1227		Levick, Harry	15/10/18
12/1366	..	Lawton, Herbert Geo. Hy.	1/7/16
235639	,,	Lake, William Edward	24/9/17
	2nd Lieut.	Malkin, N. H.	14/5/17
	2nd Lieut.	Marsden, R.	1/10/17
12/2	C.S.M.	Marsden, William	17/6/16
12/181	Pte.	Mason, Cecil Stanley	1/7/16
12/183	,,	McBride, Peter	1/7/16
12/184	,,	McNeill, Samuel Alex.	27/7/16
12/190	L/Cpl.	Moses, Fredk. Stayton	1/7/16
12/441	Pte.	Maltby, John Edwin	20/7/16
12/454	,,	Mitchell, George Alfred	17/1/17
12/568	,,	Matthews, Robert Haly Bruce	16/5/16
12/722	L/Cpl.	Macquade, Wm. Henry	1/7/16
12/736	A/Cpl.	Moulds, Harry	1/7/16
12/738	Pte.	Munro, James Bingley	6/7/16
12/985	L/Cpl.	Maclaurin, Edgar	1/7/16
12/986	Pte.	Marshall, Frank Arnold	8/8/16
12/987	,,	Marshall, Hugh	17/3/16
12/990	Cpl.	Mather, Frederick	1/7/16
12/991	Pte.	McKenzie, Alexander	4/4/16

134   History of The Sheffield City Battalion.

Reg. No.	Rank.	Name.	Date of Death.
12/992	Pte.	Medley, Harold	1/7/16
12/1000	,,	Moreton, Wm. Frederick	1/7/16
12/1002	,,	Morte, Leslie Vernon	1/7/16
12/1251	,,	Mills, Percival Fredk.	1/7/16
12/1260	,,	Millward, George Henry	17/6/17
12/1434	,	McIvor, Leonard	1/7/16
12/1478	׀	Miller, Thomas	1/7/16
12/1511		Mason, Cecil	4/7/16
12/1632		Mitchell, John Thomas	28/12/16
12/1684		Murday, Maitland	8/6/16
12/1830		Molyneux, George James	1/7/16
12/1835		Mountain, Henry	4/5/17
12/1836		Mountain, Arthur Eric Griffith	1/7/16
19224		Martin, Henry	14/11/16
28410		McNeillie, Edward	18/5/17
31326		Martin, John	27/11/16
31327		Martin, William	30/12/17
38034		Millership, J.	14/11/16
38036		Mylchrist, James	17/11/16
235216		Murphy, Walter	13/5/17
12/1379		Marshall, Harold	25/7/16
12/1607	,,	Matthewman, Wilfred	1/7/16
12/193	Sgt.	Neill, Harry	1/7/16
12/196	Pte.	Nichols, Frank	1/7/16
12/199	,,	Norris, Harold	1/7/16
12/462	,,	Naylor, Joseph	3/1/19
12/740		Newton, Leonard	1/7/16
12/1007		Newsholme, Thomas Alan Wilkinson	8/7/16
12/1009		Newton, Percy	1/7/16
38038	,,	Needham, George	12/12/16
12/208	Pte.	Owen, Geoffrey Hazlehurst	1/7/16
12/468	,,	Oliver, Thomas Wilfred	27/7/16
12/741	,,	Ortton, John Charles	20/2/15
12/1011		Oliver, Rowland	1/7/16

Roll of Honour. 135

Reg. No.	Rank.	Name.	Date of Death.
12/1013	L/Cpl.	Owen, James Shaw	9/3/17
12/1523	Pte.	Owen, Charles Edward	1/7/16
12/1014	L/Cpl.	Owen, Percy William	13/4/18
	2nd Lieut.	Perkin, P. K.	1/7/16
	2nd Lieut.	Pimm, C. W.	18/5/17
12/215	Pte.	Poile, Sidney	1/7/16
12/475	,,	Peace, Frank Herbert	1/7/16
12/480	,,	Platt, Fred	9/10/16
12/743	,,	Parker, John William	1/7/16
12/745	,,	Parr, Andrew	1/7/16
12/746	,,	Pearson, Edward	1/7/16
12/1018	Sgt.	Philbey, George	10/7/16
12/1022	Pte.	Price, Oliver	1/7/16
12/1161	L/Cpl.	Parkin, Horace George	1/7/16
12/1209	Pte.	Parsons, William Edward	1/7/16
12/1225	,,	Plant, Joseph	1/7/16
12/1315	,,	Priestley, Harry	1/7/16
12/1463	,	Pickles, John Arthur	1/7/16
12/1688	,	Potter, Albert Henry	1/7/16
12/1978	,	Phipps, Samuel	29/8/16
16879	,	Paling, Charles	4/11/16
19495	,	Parker, Henry	13/3/17
38042		Pownall, James	29/10/16
38403	,	Pennock, James	17/11/16
40031	,	Platt, Herbert	4/5/17
12/1431	,,	Pagett, William Henry	1/7/16
12/1183	,,	Plaxton, Joseph	1/7/16
12/220	Cpl.	Robertson, Alexander	1/7/16
12/488	Pte.	Rhodes, Leonard Frank	24/5/16
12/489	L/Cpl.	Rhodes, Thomas Wood	1/7/16
12/493	L/Cpl.	Rixham, Arthur	1/7/16
12/495	Pte.	Robinson, Leslie	27/7/16
12/496	Cpl.	Robinson, Philip Preston	1/7/16
12/499	L/Cpl.	Rose, George	11/4/18
12/755	Sgt.	Register, Bernard John	16/5/16
12/757	Pte.	Richards, Percy Charles	4/5/16

History of The Sheffield City Battalion.

Reg. No.	Rank.	Name.	Date of Death.
12/767	Pte.	Rodgers, Edward Gordon	4/5/16
12/1024	Cpl.	Rhodes, George Herbert	1/7/16
12/1026	Pte.	Rigg, Adam Kerr	1/7/16
12/1152	,,	Rawlin, Walter	1/7/16
12/511	,,	Shoesmith, Arnold	27/7/18
12/514	Sgt.	Simpson, Allan Arthur	1/7/16
12/516	Pte.	Slack, Alfred	16/5/16
12/523	,,	Stockill, George	1/7/16
12/525	Sgt.	Streets, John William	1/7/16
12/527	L/Cpl.	Swift, Charles Edward	18/9/16
12/771	Pte.	Saddler, Gordon Henry	1/7/16
12/772	,,	Sabben, John Clement Friend	1/7/16
12/776	,,	Sharp, Rowland Robert	1/7/16
12/781	Cpl.	Smith, Arnold Hallas	3/10/16
12/785	Pte.	Spencer, Ernest	1/7/16
12/791	,,	Stinson, Percy	1/7/16
12/795	,,	Swinscoe, Thomas Colin	1/7/16
12/1038	L/Cpl.	Salkeld, Charles Henry	1/7/16
12/1044	Pte.	Scothern, Fredk. Joseph	1/7/16
12/1045	L/Cpl.	Seaman, Robert	28/7/16
12/1050	Pte.	Simmonite, Charles	1/7/16
12/1051	L/Cpl.	Simson, Sidney	1/7/16
12/1053	Pte.	Skinner, Edmd. Seymour	1/7/16
12/1056	,,	Smith, Fred Parker	4/7/16
12/1057	L/Cpl.	Smith, Richard Elvidge	16/5/16
12/1064	Pte.	Swift, James Stuart	1/7/16
12/1127	,,	Sheldon, Samuel	1/7/16
12/1145	,,	Stubley, Thomas Wm.	16/5/16
12/1197		Stanley, John	1/7/16
12/1216		Senior, Frank Heywood	1/5/16
12/1352		Shirt, John Waters	7/7/16
12/1378		Storey, Harold	28/6/16
12/1404		Stables, Victor	18/5/17
12/1435		Scott, Walter	1/7/16
12/1480		Strickland, Joseph	16/5/16
12/1491		Stothard, Edwin Robert	1/7/16

Roll of Honour. 137

Reg. No.	Rank.	Name.	Date of Death.
12/1608	Pte.	Shaw, Tom	1/7/16
12/1549	,,	Sanderson, Edwin	22/6/17
38046	,,	Smith, William	12/5/17
40035	,,	Speight, Walter	4/5/17
12/777	,,	Shaw, Henry	22/9/17
12/793	Cpl.	Storr, George Wm.	23/4/17
12/1477	Pte.	Spencer, Horace James	15/9/16
12/1503	,,	Spencer, Joshua	16/1/16
	2nd Lieut.	Thompson, J. T.	6/8/17
12/249	Pte.	Thomas, Ernest Clifford	17/6/16
12/250	,,	Thorpe, John Leonard	1/7/16
12/251	L/Cpl.	Topham, Geo. Marshall	10/7/16
12/254	Pte.	Turner, John	1/7/16
12/528	,,	Tagg, Reginald	1/7/16
12/799	,,	Thorne, Alfred James	1/7/16
12/802	,,	Todd, Harold	3/5/16
12/804	L/Cpl.	Trickett, Andrew	1/7/16
12/805	Pte.	Tucker, Wilfred Henry Cranstone	16/5/16
12/1066	L/Cpl.	Taylor, Charles Wm.	1/7/16
12/1068	Pte.	Taylor, John William	1/7/16
12/1069	Sgt.	Thompson, Walter	1/7/16
12/1071	Pte.	Thorpe, Arthur	10/7/16
12/1073	,,	Timmons, Thomas Henry	8/11/17
12/1078	A/Sgt.	Turner, Arnold	9/3/17
12/1082	Pte.	Twigg, Benjamin	1/7/16
12/1332	,,	Taylor, Herbert	2/7/16
24249	Cpl.	Taylor, R.	19/6/17
12/1467	Pte.	Tate, Allan	1/7/16
12/1838	,,	Tuck, Jeremiah	1/7/16
23246	,,	Thorpe, Edward	31/8/16
12/1524	,,	Turton, John Alfred	1/7/16
12/1363	,,	Thompson, Arthur Henry	1/7/16
12/535	L/Cpl.	Unwin, Reg	12/4/18
12/807	Pte.	Unwin, Gilbert	4/5/16

138   History of The Sheffield City Battalion.

Reg. No.	Rank	Name	Date of Death
12/536	Pte.	Vaughton, Ernest Clifford	24/1/17
12/537	,,	Verner, Adrian	1/7/16
12/538	,,	Verner, Richard Henry	1/7/16
12/2071	,,	Vernon, Joseph Henry	10/9/16
	2nd Lieut.	Wardill, C. H.	1/7/16
	2nd Lieut.	Wilson, F. B.	7/8/16
23314	Pte.	Wood, Herbert	29/5/17
12/264	L/Cpl.	Wharton, Henry Wm.	1/7/16
12/262	Pte.	West, P. M.	12/5/17
12/265	,,	Whittaker, George	2/12/16
12/267	L/Cpl.	Wilcox, William George	25/9/17
12/272	Pte.	Wiseman, Charles	26/5/18
12/479	,,	Whittaker, William	28/7/15
12/548	A/L/Sgt.	Watkins, Francis Edwin	1/7/16
12/553	Pte.	Whitlock, Eric Francis	1/7/16
12/555	,,	Whysall, Thornton	1/7/16
12/559	L/Sgt.	Wood, Thomas Harper	2/11/16
12/809	Pte.	Waddington, William T.	1/7/16
12/812	,,	Walker, Herbert	1/7/16
12/1882	,,	Ward, George Elgie	1/7/16
12/816	,,	Wardill, Sidney George	1/7/16
12/819	,,	White, Alfred	1/7/16
12/822	,,	Wilkinson, Benj. Caswell	1/7/16
12/824	,,	Wilson, John Willie	1/7/16
12/833	Cpl.	Wright, Joseph Rodgers	1/7/16
12/1084	L/Cpl.	Walker, Fredk.	27/5/16
12/1085	Pte.	Walby, Wilfred Doubleday	9/10/17
12/1088	,,	Watson, John Owen	1/7/16
12/1090	,,	Weight, Ambrose	1/7/16
12/1097	L/Cpl.	Wilcock, Noel	1/7/16
12/1100	,,	Wilford, Cecil	14/7/16
12/1165	Pte.	Webster, Albert	1/7/16
12/1887	,,	Wainwright, Edmond	1/7/16
12/1198	,,	Williamson, Wm. Edwd.	1/7/16
12/1268		Walker, Richard Henry	16/5/16
12/1412		Wilson, Hector Atkinson	10/9/16

Roll of Honour. 139

Reg. No.	Rank.	Name.	Date of Death.
12/1484	Pte.	Waterfall, Nelson	1/7/16
12/1880	,,	White, Ronald Harry	1/7/16
28773	,,	Wilthew, Wilfred Norman	30/6/17
41628		Woodger, John Arthur	25/10/17
12/815		Ward, Charles Winn	28/8/17
12/1327		Waterhouse, John	1/7/16
12/1582		Wood, Harry	1/7/16
31342		Yelf, Robert Henry	28/10/16

Supplementary Roll of Honour

of old 12th York and Lancaster Boys killed whilst serving with other units.

Reg. No.	Rank.	Name and Unit.	Date of Death.
12/1958	Pte.	Ambler, Harry	9/7/17
12/2042	Cpl.	Atkinson, Caleb	
	Capt.	Burkett, Harold 10th K.O.Y.L.I.	5/6/17
	Pte.	Barnsley, William R., 10th Northumberland F.	25/9/16
	2nd Lieut.	Banham, Ernest, 10th East Yorks	28/9/18
1991	Pte.	Burrell, Norman Percy, 1/5th West Yorks	20/7/16
1292	L/Cpl.	Bolsover, George Frederick, 2/4 Y. and L.	23/7/18
	2nd Lieut.	Batley, A. G., 11th Manchester Regt.	27/9/18
	Lieut.	Bridgewater, E., Notts and Derby	
12/1799	Pte.	Barron, Arthur	28/3/16
27446	,,	Bingham, Richard Arthur	13/11/16
12/1936	,,	Butler, Arthur Edward	2/11/16
	2nd Lieut.	Cummins, T. C., 7th Y. and L.	25/3/18
	Capt.	Cunnington, C., R.A.M.C.	25/3/18
12/1926	Pte.	Carney, Frank Kirkby	14/8/16
30952	,,	Clarke, Frederick	21/3/18
21762	,,	Colley, George	11/3/18
	Lieut.	Derry, D. A. L., 2nd Y. and L.	9/10/16
	Pte.	Deby, Julian Thomas Henry	

Supplementary Roll of Honour. 141

Reg. No.	Rank.	Name and Unit.	Date of Death.
	Lieut.	Faker, F. L., 10th East Yorks	13/11/16
	2nd Lieut.	Furniss, C. F., 10th North Staffs Regt.	16/4/18
	Pte.	Fieldsend, Ben, Machine Gun Corps	5/4/18
1291	Cpl.	Fletcher, Sidney Stuart, 1/5 Y. and L.	13/10/18
	2nd Lieut.	Flower, W. J.	
12/1691	Pte.	Fish, George	13/4/17
	2nd Lieut.	Gould, Joseph Wm., 1/5th Y. and L.	13/10/18
	2nd Lieut.	Gilson, Edward Norman, 1/4th Y. and L.	5/11/18
	2nd Lieut.	Godwin, C. N., 10th Y. and L.	1/7/16
12/1376	Pte.	Gorrill, Robert	27/5/18
12/927	,,	Giraud, Herve A.	7/5/17
	Lieut.	Harboard, Gordon, 13th Y. and L.	26/3/18
	Cpl.	Hobson, R., 13th Y. and L.	26/3/18
	Capt.	Hipkins, Wystan F., 6th Notts and Derbys	3/10/18
	Lieut.	Honer, Douglas James	4/6/17
1647	Pte.	Holland, Albert	8/5/18
12/2041	,,	Harrison, Walter Gilbert	20/7/16
	,,	Hague, W.	1/7/16
39105	Pte.	Irons, Percy William, 13th Y. and L.	12/4/18
	2nd Lieut.	Jones, Reginald Pryce, 8th Y. and L.	19/10/17
	2nd Lieut.	Jones, G. Wm., 13th Y. and L.	12/3/18
	Lieut.	Jackson, C. A., R.A.F.	—/—/17
	L/Cpl.	Jeffcock, 7th Y. and L.	/3/18
29082	Pte.	Jones, Harry	6/6/17

Reg. No.	Rank	Name and Unit.	Date of Death.
	Capt.	Kerr, A., Notts and Derbys	15/8/18
	Pte.	Levick, Harry, 2nd Y. and L.	15/10/18
	,,	Lister, Wilfred G.	
32295	..	Lightwood, Charles Edward	29/9/18
12/1699	,,	Latham, Albert	1/7/16
	L/Cpl.	Moody, Frank, 9th Y. and L.	31/10/18
	2nd Lieut.	Munton, T., 7th Y. and L.	22/10/17
	2nd Lieut.	Morrison, A., 2nd S. Lancs.	
12/985	L/Cpl.	Maclaurin, Edgar	1/7/16
	Pte.	Naylor, Joseph, 9th Y. and L.	3/1/19
	2nd Lieut.	Nock, F. J., 9th K.O.Y.L.I	3/6/17
	2nd Lieut.	Oakes, Samuel, R.E.	6/5/17
	2nd Lieut.	Pollard, Wilfred Downes, 15th Notts and Derby	/4/18
	2nd Lieut.	Parfitt, Frank Arnold, 7th Y. and L. and R.A.F.	3/9/18
12/482	Pte.	Poole, Harold	4/7/16
1603	Pte.	Roddis, Harold, 13th Y. and L.	28/6/18
	2nd Lieut.	Robinson, Arthur Owen, Notts and Derby	21/3/18
22254	Pte.	Roberts, George Henry	17/7/16
12/1724	,,	Rhodes, Herbert	1/7/16
1313	L/Cpl.	Stenton, Albert, 2nd Y. and L.	20/5/18
	2nd Lieut.	Simpson, Herbert, 6th Notts and Derby	7/7/16
	Capt.	Simpson, Vivian, M.C., 13th Y. and L.	13/4/18
1182	Pte.	Shaw, J. G., 14th Y. and L.	1/7/16
12/1811	,,	Smedley, Harry	15/10/17
	..	Shiells, Alec. W.	1/7/16
25023		Shemeld, Edward	26/3/18

Supplementary Roll of Honour. 143

Reg. No.	Rank.	Name and Unit.	Date of Death.
	Sub-Lieut.	Taylor, Frank Arnold, Royal Naval Reserve	24/3/18
	2nd Lieut.	Thornsby, W. S., 3rd West Yorks	24/8/18
	2nd Lieut.	Townsend, J.	
12/1074	Pte.	Tingle, Arthur	9/10/17
53710	Cpl.	Uttley, Lawrence, D.L.I.	23/3/18
	Pte.	Vickers, Ernest	/16
	2nd Lieut.	Wilson, Robert, M.M., 9th Y. and L.	30/6/17
	Pte.	Williams, Evan Peter, 2nd West Yorks.	24/4/18
267		Wilcox, Wm. George, 8th Y. and L.	26/9/17
	2nd Lieut.	Whitley, Hubert, 9th D.L.I.	11/10/16
	Capt.	Woodhouse, C. H., 1/4th Y. and L.	6/6/18
12/1622	Pte.	Ward, John	1/5/18
49749	,,	Wills, Charles Alfred	21/3/18

The Memorial which was unveiled in the Sheffield Cathedral on December 20th, 1919.

APPENDIX.

(APPENDIX)

Description of the Memorial in the Sheffield Cathedral.

> The following is a brief description of the Memorial placed in the Sheffield Cathedral, and which was unveiled by Colonel C. V. Mainwaring and dedicated by Archdeacon Gresford Jones, on December 20th, 1919.

The emblem was subscribed for by surviving members of the City Battalion, and is in the form of a stone tablet with appropriate ornamentation and an inscription. The design is the work of Mr. F. Ratcliffe, A.R.I.B.A., of Sheffield, a member of the City Battalion.

The basis of the memorial is a slab of Hopton Wood stone, 4ft. by 2ft. 7in., and 3in. in thickness. This variety is quarried at Wirksworth, in Derbyshire, is of a creamy yellow colour, and takes a high polish. In the central portion a slab of Blue John is sunk flush with the face of the memorial, and superimposed on this is a bronze Calvary with medallion ornaments at the points, enamelled in gilt and red. On the left is a finely-executed bronze replica of the badge of the York and Lancaster Regiment, of which the City Battalion was the 12th fighting unit, and on the right the Sheffield City coat of arms, also carried out in bronze. These are enamelled in the requisite colours.

The lettering is incised in the stone, the surface being flush and the intervals carved out, thus showing the inscription up in relief. This reads:

"1914—1919. To the Glory of God, and to the ever glorious memory of Officers, N.C.O.s and Men of the 12th Battalion York and Lancaster Regiment (Sheffield City Battalion), who at the call of Duty and in the cause of Freedom nobly made the supreme sacrifice. This tablet is erected by the surviving members of the Battalion and dedicated on December 20th, 1919."

All the material employed in the memorial is local. The Blue John, of course, is found at Castleton, Derbyshire, and it is but rarely that a piece of such size as the one included in the tablet is unearthed. The material is so brittle and fragile to work that often good specimens are spoiled in the carving. That accident happened in the present instance a month before the delivery of the memorial, and it almost seemed as though some other medium would have to be resorted to, when the makers heard that Mr. J. W. Puttrell, F.R.G.S., the well-known geologist, had in his possession a piece of Blue John which he had treasured for years. When he was approached, Mr. Puttrell not only agreed to surrender the piece, but intimated his desire that it should be accepted as his contribution to the memory of Sheffield lads.

The whole scheme of the tablet is simple but cheerful. The designer has felt that the emblem is not consecrated merely to those who have died, and with this thesis he has striven to avoid any note of mourning. It is conceived chastely, and its main lines are straight and plain. It is a fit memorial to soldiers.—" Sheffield Daily Telegraph."

The Battalion's Poets.

As has been indicated, the early history of the Sheffield Battalion is illustrated in the poems of two of its members, who both gave their lives for freedom on 1st July, 1916.

ALEXANDER ROBERTSON was born at Edinburgh, on 12th January, 1882. He received the degree of M.A. at Edinburgh in 1906, and became B.Litt. of Oxford in 1913. In January, 1914, he joined the staff of the University of Sheffield as Lecturer in History. He enlisted in the 12th as a private, and was a corporal in "A" Company at the date of his death. Three poems of his appeared in " Soldier Poets " (Erskine Macdonald, 1916). A volume, " Comrades," is dated " Somewhere in France, May 28, 1916," and was published that year by Elkin Mathews. In 1918 the same publisher issued " Last Poems of Alexander Robertson," with a preface by Professor P. Hume Brown. In these poems one will find reflected the thoughts of a very thoughtful and cultivated man as they were called up in the different training camps of the Battalion on the voyage to Egypt, and in France.

JOHN WILLIAM STREETS, the eldest of twelve children, was a miner at Whitwell, near Mansfield, who had educated hmself to appreciate the best literature and to express his idealism in genuine poetry. A short account of him is given in " Floreamus! "—a Chronicle of the University of Sheffield, Vol. VIII, p. 73. At the time of his death he was a sergeant. He had a burning faith that England's cause was the cause of right and freedom, and he gained the reputation of being " one of the bravest men we had! " Six of his poems appeared in " Soldier Poets," and a collection called " The Undying Splendour " was issued by Mr. Erskine Macdonald in 1917. The spirit which animated the men of 1914 is nowhere shown in its unalloyed beauty better than in the works of this gifted and heroic child of the people.

www.ingramcontent.com/pod-product-compliance
Lightning Source LLC
Chambersburg PA
CBHW031144160426
43193CB00008B/249